the 23rd psalm
for the 21st century

a jewish shepherd's story

Ion solomon

purple pomegranate productions
san francisco,ca

the 23rd psalm for the 21st century
a jewish shepherd's story
by lon solomon

For more information, including reprint permission, write to:

JEWS F☼R JESUS ™
60 Haight Street
San Francisco, CA 94102
USA
jewsforjesus.org

ISBN 10: 1-881022-82-X
ISBN 13: 978-1-881022-82-4

CONTENTS

ACKNOWLEDGMENTS

I would like to say a word of thanks to some special people without whose help this book would not have been possible.

First and foremost, I would like to thank the risen Lord Jesus Christ, my Lord and Savior, who redeemed my life 38 years ago. I was self-destructing here on earth and was headed for disaster in eternity. He changed all that radically and eternally. He transformed my earthly life and made it healthy, functional and worth living. He led me into his service and illuminated my mind and heart so that I could understand his written Word. Obviously, my first and greatest expression of thanks belongs to him and him alone.

I would also like to thank Susan Perlman, my good friend, for her constant encouragement and support. Her excitement about this project inspired me to keep going and bring it to conclusion.

I would like to thank David Brickner for kindly agreeing to write the foreword for my book and for being my good friend.

Thanks also to Matt Sieger and Rebekah Harvey for their invaluable editorial help and to Paige Saunders for her creation of the unique cover.

Finally, I would like to thank my wonderful wife, Brenda, who has supported and loved me in all that the Lord has asked us to do. Next to the Lord himself, she has been my "true north" for 34 years and the greatest human blessing the Lord has ever graciously given me.

Lon Solomon
September 6, 2008

FOREWORD

Lon Solomon is the quintessential 21st century shepherd of the flock of God. Living and ministering in the capitol of the United States of America, he preaches each week in that proverbial Washington bubble. He is surrounded by people of power and influence and regularly subjected to media scrutiny and skepticism. Yet his is a megachurch not given over to the faddishness of market-driven strategies nor defined by political correctness characteristic of so many "gospel-light" institutions enamored by their own success.

Mclean Bible Church reflects the character of the man who has shepherded her growth over 30 years from a small fellowship to one of the nation's largest and most influential congregations. It is a church of warmth and love, of excellence and unyielding commitment to the truth of Scripture. Tens of thousands of people listen to Lon Solomon's sermons every week because he has a unique ability to take the truths of God's Word and make them understandable, accessible and applicable to their lives in this 21st century. How refreshing to hear the voice of a man who is sold out to Jesus, who has the courage of conviction that the Bible is the very Word of God and that the power of the gospel is sufficient for the work of the gospel.

You have in your hands a precious volume of Lon's teaching from the most popular passage of sacred Scripture, Psalm 23. You will find his interpretation sound and insightful and his application deep and convicting. Through the study of his Word, God still dramatically changes the lives of men and women today. Lon's life is an example of the power of God to change and save, and so it is an added bonus to be able to read his own personal story as part of this volume.

I have no doubt that as you read Lon's story and consider his teaching from Psalm 23, your life will be changed, your faith in God strengthened and your love for God's Word multiplied.

David Brickner
Executive Director, Jews for Jesus

PREFACE

¹The LORD *is* my shepherd;
I shall not want.
²He makes me to lie down in green pastures;
He leads me beside the still waters.
³He restores my soul;
He leads me in the paths of righteousness
For His name's sake.
⁴Yea, though I walk through the valley of the shadow
of death,
I will fear no evil;
For You *are* with me;
Your rod and Your staff, they comfort me.
⁵You prepare a table before me in the presence of
my enemies;
You anoint my head with oil;
My cup runs over.
⁶Surely goodness and mercy shall follow me all the
days of my life;
And I will dwell in the house of the LORD forever.

This book is about the most familiar six verses in the
Bible.

Many can say all or part of them by heart. Most can
pick up a Bible and find these verses with little trouble.

One cannot attend a funeral without hearing them
read or a memorial event without hearing them recited.

The 23rd Psalm may be one of the shortest psalms

but it is without a doubt one of the richest and most
beloved passages in all the Scriptures. "Blessed be the
day on which that psalm was born," said Henry Ward
Beecher. He called it "the nightingale of the psalms"
because, like that small bird, "it has filled the air of the
whole world with melodious joy, greater than the heart
can conceive."[1]

The 23rd Psalm has soothed more grief than all the
philosophies of this world put together. It has poured more
balm on hurting hearts and brought more consolation to
sorrowing people than all this world's counselors and
therapists combined. It has given hope to widows in the
night and sung to hearts that were overwhelmed with
weeping and pain. It's brought cheer to people paralyzed
by fear and doubt. Who knows how many soldiers have
died in peace as this psalm was read to them?

So we should ask the question: "What makes this little
psalm so precious, powerful and poignant in every age?
Why is it—that no matter what the circumstances are, no
matter who the individual is, no matter what the culture
may be—this psalm has been one of such dramatic impact?"

The answer, I believe, is that the 23rd Psalm focuses
on the exquisite love of God, individually and
personally, for his people. This psalm is a marvelous
reminder of how deeply and fully and tenderly God
loves every individual follower of his. That is the one
thought, the one emotion, the one feeling that
dominates every part of this psalm. As we read it we
begin to get an idea of just how deeply God has
committed himself to us—in the same way a shepherd
is committed to his dear sheep. Even in our darkest
moments and at our lowest points, this little psalm
keeps reminding us that God really does care for us,

that he really is leading us "for his name's sake" and that we need to trust that he knows what's best for us. For every vicissitude of life, this psalm is just what the doctor ordered.

This psalm wasn't written by David to be a piece of religious liturgy or a fixture at funerals and memorial services. It wasn't intended to be brought out and dusted off only in times of grief and loss. Quite the contrary. What makes this psalm so special is that it was intended to bring God's truth to bear on our everyday lives, in every age and in every culture.

My purpose in unpacking this psalm for you is very simple. I want to see God bring all of the assurance that he's put in this psalm to bear on your life. I hope when you've finished, you'll be able to reflect back and say: "My, isn't it wonderful how deeply God cares for *me*? Isn't it amazing that the Almighty God of the universe has committed himself to be *my* personal shepherd? With him as my shepherd and with the promises he's made to me in this psalm, I can face anything life brings my way and still have hope."

PART ONE

THE LORD IS MY SHEPHERD

I've been leading tours to the Holy Land since 1987. On every tour we pass flocks of sheep grazing in the desert. It looks sometimes as though they are simply wandering on their own, disorganized and directionless. Actually, however, nothing could be further from the truth. If one looks carefully, one will always see the shepherd standing and watching over the sheep. He's there to lead them, to protect them, to provide for them and to tend to their every need. There is a sense of security and calm that dominates the whole scene simply because of the presence of the shepherd.

Notice how David begins the 23rd Psalm: "The Lord is my shepherd."

There are two key words here. The first word is "my" and the second word is "shepherd."

First, David begins by saying that the Lord is *my* shepherd. This is an amazing statement. David did not say, "The Lord is the shepherd of the whole earth." He didn't say, "The Lord is the shepherd of all Israel" or, "the shepherd of everybody in the universe."

David declared, "The Lord is *my* shepherd." What a sweet word. In fact, I believe that this is probably the most significant word in the whole psalm. It conveys the personal warmth, the intimacy and the deep relationship that runs through the entire psalm.

Take a highlighter or a pen and go through this psalm and underline every reference to "me," "mine," "my" or "I." You'll be fascinated when you do for what you'll find is that in six short verses, these words are used sixteen times. What David is trying to point out to us is the depth of love and commitment that God has, not to the world, not to the human race in general, but to you and me as his individual sheep. It's this sense of personal assurance that gives the 23rd Psalm its power.

David begins this psalm by saying, "Look, if God is a shepherd to nobody else in the world, I'll tell you something: he's a shepherd to *me*. He cares about *me*. He loves *me*. He's committed to *me*. He's made some awesome promises to *me*."

Thirty centuries later, if we're one of God's sheep, what God wants to communicate to us in this word "my" is that he loves you and me today just the way he loved David. God wants us to *know* that this is how he feels about us. He wants us to be surer of his love for us as individuals than we are of our own names.

Secondly, I want us to notice in this first verse the word "shepherd." The Lord is my *shepherd*. Now I've thought a lot about why David chose this word. Out of all the images David could have chosen to describe how God feels about his people, why did he choose the word "shepherd"?

I suggest that one of the reasons is that David was a shepherd himself. He understood the unique relationship between a shepherd and his sheep, a relationship like no other relationship anywhere in the natural world.

We don't know exactly when David wrote this psalm. Maybe it was in his younger days, sitting up on the hillside, looking over his sheep and just thinking. Perhaps it was a quiet moment. Perhaps he had just finished rescuing one of his sheep from a predator or bringing a wandering sheep back to the fold. And as he was sitting and thinking about his sheep and his intimate connection to them, perhaps the thought hit him: "You know what? That's exactly how God is connected to me."

Or maybe it was later in his life, when David was the king of Israel that he wrote this psalm. Perhaps one morning he got up and looked out his window and saw shepherds leading their flocks out to their fields for the day. Maybe standing there at his window, David mused: "You know what? The way those shepherds lead and care for those sheep—my, that's exactly how God leads and cares for me. And I understand this because I used to do that very same thing for *my* sheep years ago."

Who knows when David wrote this psalm? But whenever he wrote it, David chose the word "shepherd" because he understood what being a shepherd meant.

But there's more to it than just that. For you see, not only did David understand this relationship between a shepherd and his sheep, but he also knew that everyone in Israel who read this psalm would understand this imagery too. Shepherds covered the landscape in ancient Israel. If you weren't one yourself, you knew people who were and did business with them on a weekly basis. *Everybody* in Israel instinctively understood the role of a shepherd in relation to his sheep. No further explanations were needed.

Unfortunately, today in the 21st century, there are very few of us who still naturally understand this shepherding imagery. If the 23rd Psalm began with "The Lord is my life coach" or "The Lord is my personal trainer," no one would have to explain that imagery any further. If the psalm began, "The Lord is my software and I am the hardware," we'd all get the unique implications and connotations that flow through this word picture. But I'm afraid most of us today don't connect as readily with "The Lord is my shepherd."

So in order for us to appreciate the depth and richness that David built into the 23rd Psalm when he declared, "The Lord is my shepherd," we need to familiarize ourselves with the unique relationship between shepherds and sheep in ancient Israel.

First of all, we need to realize that shepherds take total responsibility for the life of their sheep. Sheep are not like most other animals. Turn a sheep loose in the wilderness and it will die. Take a sheep and let it go free in the woods and it will die. More than any other class of livestock, sheep require endless attention and meticulous, round-the-clock care.

The reason is that sheep are essentially helpless and stupid animals. They can't provide for their own food like lions and tigers. They can't defend themselves from predators. They've got no speed. They've got no strength. They have no natural weapons for defense like claws or teeth. They can't climb trees. They can't dig tunnels. They can't swim across rivers. They have no camouflage. Sheep are easily frightened. They're literally scared of their own shadow. And to make matters worse, sheep are notoriously stubborn and ornery, so that even when people try to help them, they often resist and rebel.

Above all this, sheep have an incredibly poor sense of direction. If a sheep gets lost, it will simply lie down. It won't even try to find its way back home. I mean, Benji they're not! Unless a shepherd goes out and finds that sheep, a lost sheep is a dead sheep.

The point of all this is that, because of the kind of creatures that sheep are, a shepherd ends up with the *total* responsibility for the lives of his sheep. Every moment of every day, a shepherd must be on active duty. If he were to relax his diligent care for his sheep for even a few moments, a shepherd could easily lose some of his sheep. So in agreeing to be our shepherd, Almighty God has agreed that he will provide this kind of total, all-consuming, 24/7, 365-day-a-year care for us, just like a human shepherd does for his sheep.

Second, for a *good* shepherd, the welfare of his sheep is his total and ultimate goal in life. A good shepherd has no greater reward and no higher joy than to see his sheep contented and well cared for. And he's willing to pay for this result with his own life, if need be. He's willing to give up his own personal comfort and pleasure from sunup to sundown and all through the night in order to bring about the well-being of his sheep. A good shepherd lays his life on the line for his sheep, and he's happy to do so because of the value that the sheep have in his eyes.

How well any given group of sheep fare is directly related to what kind of shepherd they have. Sheep who have a gentle, kind, brave and sacrificial shepherd—those sheep prosper. Conversely, sheep that have a cruel, cowardly and selfish shepherd—those sheep deteriorate.

Jesus said in John 10:10–11: "I came that they may have life, and have it abundantly. I am the good shepherd; the good shepherd lays down His life for the sheep."

In agreeing to be our personal shepherd, God has agreed to be a *good* shepherd and to treat us in the exact way such a shepherd treats his sheep. He has agreed to give his life in order for us to prosper and be safe as his sheep. He has agreed to personally intervene in our lives to see to it that we are thriving and flourishing. **In short, God has committed himself to *our* highest welfare as *his* highest priority**.

Third, not only is a good shepherd someone who takes total responsibility for his sheep and who dedicates his entire life for the welfare of his sheep. A good shepherd also builds an intimate relationship between himself and each of his sheep.

There is an intimacy that grows up between a shepherd and his sheep like no other between man and animal in the natural world. It's not just that each sheep is so valuable to the shepherd. It's not just that the shepherd pours his whole life into caring for the sheep. For sure, these truths form a natural bond between the shepherd and his sheep. But even beyond that, there is a mysterious union that forms. There is a mystical bonding that occurs. The shepherd and the sheep literally become "family." F. W. Robertson, a famous English preacher, commented on this:

> Beneath the burning skies and the clear starry nights of Palestine there grows up between the shepherd and his flock an union of attachment and tenderness . . . a kind of friendship. . . . Alone in those vast solitudes with no human being near, the shepherd and the sheep feel a life in common. . . . Between them there is woven by night and day, by summer suns and winter frosts, a living network of sympathy. The greater and the less mingle their being together: they feel each other. "The shepherd knows his sheep, and is known of them."[2]

This relationship and linkage that develops between a shepherd and his sheep is unique in the world of men and animals. This same closeness never develops between a farmer and his cows or a rancher and his horses or a Bedouin and his camels. But there's a union between a shepherd and his sheep that make them "family."

This being true, it means that a person cannot be a good shepherd and remain aloof from his sheep. It is simply not possible. And everyone in Israel reading David's psalm would have immediately understood this.

When God agreed to be our shepherd and to take us on as his personal sheep, he agreed to build such a relationship with each of us—a relationship of "family." God agreed to open himself up to us and relate to us on this level of personal intimacy. He agreed to permit us into his soul and to let us know him in a way that the rest of the world will never know him. He agreed to allow us to explore the depths and riches of who God is. We're talking about Almighty God making himself vulnerable and exposed to us so that we can truly begin to grasp his essential nature and being. This is what Jesus meant when he said that a shepherd "is known by his sheep."

What all this means is that God takes a risk when he agrees to be our shepherd. He risks the fact that you and I might hurt him, because there's always that risk when we open ourselves up to another person.

And we do hurt God, don't we? How many times does the Bible talk about the fact that we as his sheep grieve the heart of God? For example, referring to the Israelites and their disobedient behavior in the wilderness after the Exodus, God says in Psalm 95:10: "For forty years I was grieved with that generation." When God saw that the inclination of mankind's hearts was toward evil continually in the days before Noah's flood, the Bible says in Genesis 6:6: "The LORD was sorry that He had made man on the earth." And Paul tells those who are followers of Christ that they can "grieve the Holy Spirit" (Ephesians 4:30) by their disobedient behavior.

We must understand that the only reason it is possible for us to bring grief and sadness to the heart of God is because he has allowed his heart to be exposed and vulnerable to us. Because of his commitment to intimacy with us as his sheep, he has given us the platform from which we can hurt him and make him sad. God did this voluntarily. He didn't have to do so. He could have forgiven us for our wrongdoings and agreed to take us to heaven without ever exposing himself to us at all. He could have remained aloof and detached. But he didn't, because that's not what it means to be a shepherd.

I was reading an article in *TIME* magazine about *Platoon*, the Vietnam War movie that is regarded as the most realistic portrayal of what it was like to have fought in that war. According to the *TIME* article, in Vietnam there was a curious behavior pattern that developed regarding fresh soldiers arriving from America. When these new recruits got there, nobody wanted to know their names. They just referred to these men as "fresh meat." The veterans didn't want to know where they came from or if they had a girlfriend back home. They didn't want to know if they were married or had children. They just didn't want to know them personally at all.

The reason for this, according to *TIME*, is because so many of these new soldiers got killed in the first few weeks they were there. For the veteran soldiers to have known these men intimately or to have gotten involved in their lives would have brought them that much more pain at their death. This way, when they put these men in body bags, the veterans could do so without emotion. Their aloofness was simply a way to protect themselves.

Now God could have protected himself against us in

this very same way. If all that mattered to God were his own emotional safety and comfort, he would never have let you and me into his soul like a shepherd does his sheep. He'd be crazy to do this, because we are always falling short, always letting him down, always doing and saying things that disappoint and hurt God.

But, you see, this is the whole point: we matter more to God than even his own comfort. That's why God opened himself up to us like a shepherd. That's why he says to us: "Come on in and connect deeply with me. I'm going to be your shepherd and you're going to be MY sheep. And I know I'm going to get hurt but it's all right. Because I'm going to love you unconditionally even when you hurt me—just like a shepherd does with his sheep. Come on in and we'll do this thing called 'life' together."

In summary, this then is what David was saying when he declared that "The Lord is my shepherd":

1. God has agreed to take total responsibility for our safety, welfare, care and prosperity as his sheep.
2. God has agreed to invest his life in us as his sheep without measure.
3. God has agreed to open himself up to us as his sheep and allow us to explore the depths of who he is as God in genuine intimate relationship.

When David called God his "shepherd," every person in Israel realized the depth of all these implications.

When I became a father at age 28, I had no idea what I was getting myself into. I think most parents would say the same thing. In fact, if most parents had really known what was coming, they'd have been scared to do it. The totality of the responsibility is awesome.

I'm not saying that I regret being a father. Quite the opposite—I love it. What I'm trying to say is that being a good parent is a little bit like being a good shepherd. We agree to take total responsibility for another person (at least while they are under our roof). We agree to invest our lives in this other person without measure. And we agree to open ourselves up to this person and allow him or her to become so intimately connected to us that they can hurt us in a way that no other person can. Being a parent, like being a shepherd, means a lot of plain old hard work and a level of naked commitment to another person that is positively staggering.

But, you know, when God agreed to be our shepherd, he did not enter into that commitment in the same way I entered into being a father. He knew, ahead of time, every nook and cranny of what he was getting himself into. He knew what an awesome demanding responsibility he was taking on. He understood that he was accepting total liability for our life, our care and our ultimate well-being. He realized that, just like sheep, we are often undependable, unfaithful and disobedient and that we were going to hurt and grieve him many times over.

God knew exactly what he was getting into and yet he wasn't scared away. No, as a matter of fact, God willingly said: "I want that responsibility. I'll take that responsibility. I'll bear the cost gladly. Please let me be your personal shepherd. Please agree to become one of MY personal sheep."

The one thing I want us to walk away with after reading this book is the realization that when God entered into being our shepherd—with all the promises and commitments on his part that the rest of Psalm 23 is going to explain to us—he got into it with his eyes wide open. He decided to be our shepherd because he loves us, pure and simple. There's no other logical reason why God would do this except for that. He loves you and he loves me.

The Bible says that when Jesus saw the crowds, "they were distressed and dispirited like sheep without a shepherd" (Matthew 9:36). Nothing has changed in twenty centuries. Today, people are still distressed and dispirited. They're still defenseless, fearful, faint and wandering aimlessly. Sometimes, on top of all this, they're stubborn and hardheaded. We are sheep!

None of us ever voluntarily decided to be sheep. This is simply our nature. God did not come to us as the human race and say, "Hey, would y'all like to be sheep or tigers? Make a choice." That never happened. We are sheep, period. That's just the way it is.

The only one who had any choice in all this was God. He had the choice of whether he wanted to be our shepherd or not. He could have said, "Are you kidding? I'm not getting involved with folks like this. Let them go their own way. Let them run around in a circle. Let them go out there and get themselves lost or hurt or killed. Let them be torn up by predators. Let anything happen to them that wants to happen, but I don't want to get near these folks with all their needs and problems."

God could have made that choice. And, if he had made that choice, neither you, nor I, nor all the angels could have changed God's mind. God had the choice of deciding, totally as a function of his own free will, whether he wanted to enter into this shepherd-sheep relationship with us as human beings.

So let's conclude by asking: "Why did God make this decision? Why did he voluntarily offer to become our shepherd?"

Well, the answer is found in Matthew 9:36: "Seeing the people, He [Jesus] felt compassion for them, because they

were distressed and dispirited like sheep without a
shepherd." When God looks at us and sees what helpless
sheep we are, his response is compassion. His response
could be a number of other things—disgust, anger, rejection
and revulsion—but it's not. It's compassion! And this is the
only reason why God offers to be a personal shepherd for
each one of us: because in the deepest recesses of his heart,
God truly and eternally loves every human being alive.

The richness of what God communicates to us here in
verse 1 is incredible. Every day we go out into this world
as helpless sheep. But the great news is that we're not
going out without a shepherd. The Lord of the universe is
going out with us, determined to lead us, protect us,
provide for us and refresh us no matter what the world
system throws our way. So how cool is that?

We didn't earn God being our shepherd. We didn't
deserve it. We didn't merit it nor are we worthy of it.
God chose to do this for us because he loves us. And all
we can do is say, "Lord, thank you! It's the greatest
comfort in the world to know that you are my shepherd."

*Dear Father, thank you for your amazing love for us.
It is a love that we do not deserve nor have we earned. It
is a love that you bestow on us utterly as a function of
your mercy and your grace.*

*But it is a real love. It is a deep and compassionate
love. It is a self-sacrificing and eternal love. It is a love like
a shepherd has for his sheep, which causes him to give his
life for the sheep.*

*Lord, may we live our whole lives with the constant
realization of your great "shepherd love" for us. May it
dominate our worldview and encourage our souls every
day of our lives. In Jesus' name, we pray. Amen!*

PART TWO

I SHALL NOT WANT

Years ago, after I preached part one of this verse as a sermon at McLean Bible Church, my wife said, "Could I give you a little piece of advice?"

"You know," she said, "I really enjoyed that message, 'The Lord is My Shepherd.' It just seemed to me that you stretched it out a little more than you needed to. At this rate, it'll take you forever to get through this psalm!"

I said, "Maybe you're right. I'll see if I can't cover more ground and keep it shorter in the next message."

Well, I did try. However, all I got done the next week was the phrase "I shall not want."

It's not that I was trying to stretch out my treatment of this psalm unnecessarily. It's just that there's too much imbedded in every phrase to hurry through it. And in the same way, I want us to take our time in dealing with this psalm, so we are sure to extract all the wonderful truth that David built into it.

In part one, we focused on the opening phrase of Psalm 23, "The Lord is my shepherd." We saw that there were two key words in that phrase, "my" and "shepherd." And now that we understand the powerful imagery that lies behind God being our personal shepherd, it's time to turn our attention on what this truth really means in our everyday life.

The first outworking of God being my shepherd is simply "I shall not want." The Hebrew word translated "want" here literally means "to lack; to be in want."

This verse is not saying that, because God is my shepherd, I will never want or desire something in life. It's saying that I won't have any true needs that God as my heavenly shepherd won't meet. It means that I won't have any areas of my life where I am lacking what I need to be healthy, safe and prosperous. It means that there is nothing that I genuinely need that my shepherd will not provide for me.

This is what David is really declaring. David declares that there will never be a moment in life—ever—when we truly need something that God won't supply.

Now David was not the first person in history to understand this great reality about God's care for his people.

Moses observed this same truth some 450 years before David, when he said to the Israelites, "These 40 years [in the wilderness] the LORD your God has been with you; you have not lacked a thing" (Deuteronomy 2:7). And it's interesting to note that Moses uses the same Hebrew word for "lack" as David uses, translated as "want," in Psalm 23. Later, in Deuteronomy 8:9, Moses says that once the Israelites are in the Promised Land, they "will not lack anything." Same Hebrew word again.

In fact, one has to wonder if David didn't have these words of Moses in mind when he wrote this verse in Psalm 23. Personally, I'm certain that David did. The correlation between David's words and Moses' words is simply too striking to be coincidental. And this is significant, because it tells me that David was a student of God's written Word—that he read the Bible and meditated

on it. It tells me that he had internalized the Bible and
knew its truths about God's character well enough to
have it flow out of his own writings spontaneously.

Now, the expression "I shall not want" is really the
keynote of the 23rd Psalm. The rest of the psalm is
simply an expanding upon, a drawing out from, and an
amplifying of, this phrase, "I shall not want." In other
words, the five verses that follow are merely David
explaining to us all the different ways in which God
makes sure that we as his sheep never want.

Now you might say, "So, Lon, does this verse mean
that I will never have trouble in my life? Does it mean that
I will never experience failure, heartache, tragedy or loss?
Is that what David is saying here?" The answer is no,
absolutely no. God's sheep always have faced and always
will face adversity in life, just like real sheep do. In fact,
we're told in the Bible that David's own sheep faced
enormous challenges. David mentions in 1 Samuel 17:34
that there were many times when lions or bears came
and took a lamb from his flock and David had to go
rescue that lamb. David himself said in Psalm 34:19,
"Many are the afflictions of the righteous."

When God is my shepherd, this does not mean that I
am exempt from all difficulties and dangers. What provided
David's sheep with security and hope was not the *absence*
of ravenous lions and prowling bears but the *presence* of
David as the shepherd to protect and rescue them. The
same is true for us today—what provides us today with
security and confidence is not the *absence* of danger and
difficulty but the *presence* of the Great Shepherd.

Now it's certainly true that, because of the Great
Shepherd's presence, many times we are able to avert
danger altogether. This happens when sheep listen to
the voice of their shepherd and follow his guidance.

This happens when we listen to God's voice and follow his guidance as given to us in the Scriptures. This is why the Bible refers to itself in Psalm 119:105 as "a lamp to my feet and a light to my path." Again in Psalm 119:130: "The unfolding of Your words gives light; it gives understanding to the simple." This is why David said in Psalm 119:104, "From Your precepts I get understanding; Therefore I hate every false way."

In this same vein, David declared in Psalm 19:7–11:

The law of the LORD is perfect, restoring the soul;
The testimony of the LORD is sure, making wise the simple. . . .
The commandment of the LORD is pure,
enlightening the eyes. . . .
The judgments of the LORD are true; they are
righteous altogether. . . .
Moreover, by them Your servant is warned; In
keeping them there is great reward.

The point of all these statements is this: God's promise that "I shall not want" will often mean that I don't experience a large amount of failure or tragedy or loss or heartache or hurt. It will often mean that I avoid a lot of difficulties and dangers that other people fall into.

And the reason for this is that my Great Shepherd has given me a guidebook for life, to help me make wise choices that insulate me from so many harmful eventualities and to warn me to steer clear of disaster. This is one of the ways that God fulfills his commitment to me that "I shall not want."

Now, all this presupposes that I am paying attention to God's guidebook and making my choices in life according to its tenets. Even as God's sheep, when I fail to do this, I can quickly end up in trouble.

But we must be quick to add that all trouble that strikes our lives as God's sheep is not automatically because we made bad choices. There are times when God allows tough things to enter our lives simply as part of his sovereign plan for us. That was certainly the case for Job, Joseph, Daniel and other Old Testament heroes of the faith.

When this happens, as part of God's commitment that we "shall not want," God comes and rescues us. This is why David said in Psalm 34:6: "This poor man cried, and the LORD heard him and saved him out of all his troubles."

I can't even begin to count the number of times this has happened in my life. So often, I turn around and find myself in the middle of dangerous situations that threaten my well-being and my safety. Sometimes this is the result of my own doing, when I have disregarded God's tenets in the Bible and, like a dumb sheep, wandered off from the Lord into places where I have no business being.

Other times, it's no fault of my own—I'm just wandering along when suddenly I realize I'm on precarious ground and in need of rescuing.

Either way, my first reaction in these moments is always the same: I cry out to my heavenly shepherd like a lamb in danger cries out to his human shepherd.

In case after case like this, God has intervened in the circumstances of life for me as his sheep and rescued me. This is exactly what David did for his sheep when a lion or a bear abducted one of them—David went and picked that lamb up and carried him back to safety. And there are many times when this is exactly what our heavenly shepherd does for us.

There's a second way, however, that God sometimes

rescues his sheep from trouble. You see, there are times when, for our own growth and spiritual development, God knows that we must go *through* a situation and not around it. Psalm 23, verse 1, is telling us that when these times happen God promises he will be right there next to us, making sure we don't fall or fail.

In other words, rather than always taking us *out of* danger, sometimes God takes us *through* danger by providing his supernatural presence and his supernatural comfort and his supernatural inner strength to see us through.

Any parent can relate to both of these ways of providing deliverance.

Sometimes we find our child in a situation where we decide the best thing to do is to simply inject ourselves into that situation and extricate our child out of it.

Other times, however, such as when a child is facing a big test at school, or a big tryout for an athletic team or a cheerleading squad or a big performance or recital—we as parents realize that our child needs to face this challenge and go through it. What we give them to help deliver them in this stressful situation, then, is not extrication but our personal presence—holding their hand, praying with them, reassuring them, encouraging them and providing every kind of support they need to soothe away the anxiety and help them go through the situation honorably and successfully.

It's the Great Shepherd himself who decides, unilaterally, whether we as his sheep need to go *through* a given situation or *around* it. That decision belongs to the shepherd alone. Were that option given to us as the sheep, we would *always* choose to go around every difficult situation. That's just the way we're wired as human beings. But the fact is that the final choice is never ours. We can pray and ask our heavenly shepherd to choose that option, but the final decision always rests with him.

Either way, whether the Lord chooses for us to go around or through some difficulty, his promise is exactly the same: "I shall not want." Whatever I need to go through or around a problem, God promises that he is going to always provide it for me. That's what David is really saying here.

Now, what are some of the practical ways in everyday life that the Good Shepherd takes care of us so that we "do not want"? How does he make sure that we have all we need to live a healthy, functional life?

Well, the Bible tells us about six major ways in which God sees to this.

Way number one: **God guides his sheep.** Earlier in this chapter we spoke about this way. But let's reiterate it.

A literal sheep is in greatest danger when it is separated from the rest of the flock and walking on paths that are precipitous. This same thing is true of God's sheep. This is why God gave us the Bible—to provide us with day-by-day and moment-by-moment spiritual guidance. In Psalm 32:8, God promises his sheep that "I will instruct you and teach you in the way which you should go; I will counsel you with My eye upon you." In Proverbs 3:5–6, God says, "Trust in the LORD with all your heart and do not lean on your own understanding. In all your ways acknowledge Him, and *He will make your paths straight.*"

This is the first and most basic way in which God makes sure that we live healthy, functional lives. Through the truth of the Bible, he guides our steps so that we will stay on the straight and narrow path of biblical choices and behavior. Through the truth of the Bible, he also convicts us of any disobedient behavior in our personal lives that has put us in harm's way.

This is a huge form of protection for us as God's sheep, for if we listen and respond to God's promptings in this arena, and we stay close to home spiritually, we will simply avoid those solitary spiritual places where we end up becoming exposed to danger and harm.

In reflecting back on my more than three decades of being one of God's sheep, I can see this truth in spades. Every time I chose to obey God's guidance found in the commands of the Bible and the promptings of his Spirit in my heart, I avoided troubles that other people fell into. Conversely, every time I chose to go in a direction contrary to where God was guiding me by his Word and his Spirit, I ended up needing to be rescued from some trouble or crisis that my poor choices had gotten me into.

One of the chief ways in which God makes sure that "we do not want"—that we have what we need to live healthy lives—is by providing solid spiritual guidance for us in the Bible and in the inner working of his Spirit. By following that guidance, we simply avoid, as much as is possible in a sin-infested world, those places where we can find ourselves in danger.

Way number two: God seeks his sheep when they wander away. Sometimes, even in spite of God's guidance, we as sheep simply decide to wander away spiritually and get ourselves in trouble. It's simply part of our basic nature as sheep.

Or sometimes predators come right into the flock and grab us and lead us away into places of great jeopardy. These can be friends at school, acquaintances at work or anyone who encourages us to make choices that are contrary to God's instructions in the Bible.

In those times God uses a different mechanism to take care of us: he goes personally and seeks out his lost and endangered sheep.

God says in Ezekiel 34:11–12: "Behold, I Myself will search for My sheep and seek them out. As a shepherd cares for his herd in the day when he is among his scattered sheep, so I will care for My sheep and will deliver them from all the places to which they were scattered."

In one of the most famous imageries of the Bible in Matthew 18, Jesus presents himself as the shepherd who leaves the 99 sheep and goes into the mountains seeking the one sheep that has gone astray. And in the parallel account in Luke 15, it says that the shepherd seeks that sheep until he finds it. Jesus doesn't give up. And when he does find the lost sheep, Luke 15:5 says, "He lays it on his shoulders, rejoicing" and carries it back to the flock. This scene is one of the most painted scenes in all of Christian art: Jesus, the Great Shepherd, carrying his lost sheep back to safety on his shoulders.

But God wants us to understand that this is more than just a beautiful metaphor for artists to illustrate. This is part of God's commitment to his sheep. It's another way in which the Great Shepherd fulfills his promise that "I shall not want."

How does God seek lost sheep in our world today and bring them back to the safety of the fold? Well, he does it in a variety of ways.

God seeks us by the Holy Spirit's convicting ministry directly to our souls, whereby our conscience begins to scream out that we are following the wrong pathways in life.

God seeks us by sending parents, friends and even strangers across our path who pray for us and speak to us about our need to make a U-turn and return to God.

God seeks us by having us bump into radio broadcasts or podcasts or TV programs or sermon tapes or Christian books or pamphlets that pierce our hardness of heart, testifying to us that we are living on dangerous ground and urging us to restore our walk with God.

My friend, if you're one of God's sheep, and you've wandered away from the fold, you can be absolutely certain that God is out there seeking to bring you home. He wants to pick you up with all your woundedness, lay you gently on his shoulders and carry you to safety. He wants to "make up to you for the years that the swarming locust has eaten" (Joel 2:25). And he'll do this for you as soon as you'll let him.

This is just another way that God fulfills his promise that "I shall not want."

Way number three: God provides daily bread for his sheep.

Isaiah 40:11 says, "Like a shepherd He will tend [feed] His flock." As I read these words, I think of that haunting melody in the oratorio *Messiah*, where the alto and soprano soloists stand together and sing. The alto begins with, "He shall feed His flock like a shepherd." Then the soprano comes in singing, "Come unto Him all ye that labor and are heavy laden, and He will give you rest."

They go back and forth in a melodic harmony that I believe is the most gripping moment in the entire oratorio. And what makes it so gripping is that they are singing about the very heart of God for his sheep.

Psalm 34:9 says, "O fear the LORD, you His saints; for to those who fear Him there is no want. The young lions do lack and suffer hunger; but they who seek the LORD shall not be in want of any good thing."

When I was a student at the University of North Carolina Chapel Hill in the late 1960s, I wanted to hitchhike around the country, but I was too afraid. I'd seen the movie *Easy Rider* (it's a classic now but it was current then!) where they blow these guys up with shotguns. And since my hair was long, I decided there was way too much danger out there.

But then I gave my life to Jesus in 1971 and I knew I was going to heaven if somebody blew me away. I had no wife, no children, no job and no responsibilities. All I had was a dog! I figured if I was ever going to do it, now was the moment. So I sold everything I owned, bought a knapsack and a sleeping bag and set off with my dog, Noah, to see America.

When I left Chapel Hill in April 1971, I had $5 in my pocket. That was it. I decided that I was going to be a missionary as I hitchhiked around, so I carried a wad of gospel pamphlets with me and I gave them to the drivers who picked me up. As a result, I had some great opportunities to share the Lord with people all over America for the next six months.

I just went out there on the road and said, "Lord, I've got nothing but my dog and I guess, if it gets really bad, I can eat him! And I'm going to put you to the test here and see if you can really meet the needs of your sheep supernaturally, all by yourself."

When I finally arrived in Washington, D.C., in October of that year, I had not worked a day in six months, but I still had $5 in my pocket. I had never missed a meal nor had my dog. People had graciously fed the two of us, given us money and provided places for us to shower and sleep. It just happened as I walked every day relying on God.

This was a great experience for me at the beginning of my Christian life. It taught me that God can be trusted to meet the material needs of his sheep. I may not have possessed everything I wanted during those six months— like maybe a little more air-conditioning on some days! But I never wanted for a thing that I really needed. You can read in greater detail how I came to know the Lord in part two of this book.

Maybe you've never been in a situation like the one I described, and I'm sad if you haven't. Because it's when we're in situations where Jesus is all we've got, we discover that Jesus is all we really need anyway.

David had learned this. Look at what he said in Psalm 37:25: "I have been young and now I am old, yet I have not seen the righteous forsaken or his descendants begging bread." David doesn't say that sometimes we as God's sheep don't get close to this point in our lives. But David declares that God always, without fail, steps in and provides, so that His sheep "shall not want."

This is God's promise to every one of us as his sheep. This is why Jesus said, "do not be worried about your life, as to what you will eat or what you will drink; nor for your body, as to what you will put on. . . . your heavenly Father knows that you need all these things. But seek first His kingdom and His righteousness, and all these things will be added to you" (Matthew 6:25, 32–33).

God supplies all our material needs. This is just another way that the Great Shepherd makes sure that his sheep "do not want."

***Way number four*: God carries the weak sheep in his arms.**

I really love this one because I've experienced it so many times. When we're feeble and we can't walk anymore on our own, the Bible says that God carries us in his arms. He personally takes care of the lame and weak sheep.

Isaiah 40:11 says: "Like a shepherd He will tend His flock, in His arm He will gather the lambs and carry them in His bosom; He will gently lead the nursing ewes." In a flock, there are two categories of sheep that always have trouble keeping up: the young, feeble lambs and the sheep that are pregnant. A good and tender shepherd always gives special care to these sheep. David himself had no doubt spent many an hour carrying a lamb or two in his arms when they had become too tired or weak to keep going.

The Bible declares that these are the human sheep in whom God likewise takes a special interest. God constantly bears feeble and hurting sheep in his arms and carries them next to his chest when they can't keep up.

Now, no matter how long we have been followers of Christ, every one of us, from time to time, fits into this category. We may have been strong and stable in our walk with God for years. But it's amazing, when adverse circumstances strike, how quickly we can be reduced to weary lambs that can't keep up anymore.

I know I can certainly relate to this and I'll bet you can too.

I was a seminary graduate, a follower of Christ for over twenty years, a seminary professor for five years and had been a pastor for twelve years when our daughter, Jill, was born with a serious genetic disorder called mitochondrial disease. She quickly began having multiple uncontrolled seizures every day. She suffered severe brain injury from the more than 5,000 grand mals that she has had. Today, she is unable to speak, dress herself or take care of her own toileting. If she were to wander outside on a winter day without a coat and become cold, she would not realize why she was feeling cold nor would she know to come inside and get a coat.

When Jill was born in 1992, I knew the Bible well in both Greek and Hebrew. I had preached over a thousand sermons. And yet, within a few months of the beginning of my daughter's illness, I was reduced to a weak and feeble lamb. And I know what it's like to have the Great

Shepherd scoop me up in his arms and tenderly carry me as I hugged him for dear life.

I love the little poem called "Footprints." Let me paraphrase it. A man dreamed that he was walking down the beach with the Lord. Across the sky flashed scenes from the man's life. For many scenes, the man notices that there were two sets of footprints in the sand—one his and one God's. And this gave the man great solace to know that the Lord was always walking beside him.

But the man also noticed that, in those moments when his life had been the toughest, there was only one set of footprints in the sand.

This bothered the man and he said to the Lord, "Lord, you said that once I decided to follow you, you'd never leave me alone. But I see that during the most difficult times in my life, there is only one set of footprints. I don't understand. Why, when I needed you the most, did you abandon me?"

And God replied, "My precious child, during those times of deep suffering, when you see only one set of footprints, it was then that I carried you."

This is what the Great Shepherd does for his sheep: when we need to be carried, he carries us. When you feel like you're a feeble lamb who can't keep up anymore, let me tell you what to do. You tell the Great Shepherd that you want to hop into his arms—and he'll let you.

This is just another way that God sees to it that we "shall not want."

***Way number five*: God knows every one of his sheep personally.**

In John 10:14, Jesus says: "I am the good shepherd, and I *know* My own." In 2 Timothy 2:19, Paul says: "The Lord *knows* those who are His." A good earthly shepherd knows every one of his sheep individually. Every sheep has a different personality. Every sheep has its own peculiarities and its own eccentricities. A good earthly shepherd makes it his business to learn the unique characteristics of every sheep in his flock. He learns their quirks, their weird habits and their likes and dislikes. He learns how to lead and positively motivate every sheep individually based on its unique qualities. He doesn't handle one sheep the way he handles another sheep, because they are each unique and special creatures.

Now, the Good Shepherd treats us, his sheep, in the very same way. He knows every one of us through and through. He knows our likes and our dislikes. He knows our weaknesses and our strengths. He knows every one of our wrinkles and warts. He knows just what each one of us needs—uniquely and individually—for our potential for God to be maximized.

And so our Good Shepherd mixes up a recipe for life that is made to order for every one of his sheep. He adds a little bit of testing, a spoonful of success, a dash of failure, a pinch of heartache, a cup of joy, mixes it all in the casserole dish of his presence and heats it with the power of his Spirit. The recipe God uses for you is one that belongs to no one else but you, because he knows you utterly and completely, better even than you know yourself. And the Good Shepherd never makes a mistake. He never gives you anybody else's recipe nor does he give anybody else your recipe.

This is why Jeremiah 29:11 says, "'For I know the plans that I have for YOU,' declares the LORD, 'plans for welfare and not for calamity to give YOU a future and a hope.'" God creates the recipe for life for every one of his sheep individually. And do you know what this means? It means that we can trust him. It means that, whatever the Good Shepherd sends our way in life, he knows exactly what he's doing. He hasn't made a mistake, because he knows you too well. He knows exactly what you need and that's exactly what he's mixed and sent to you.

I shall never want because God knows everything about me and always gives me what I really need to be fulfilled, healthy and productive for his glory.

Way number six: God has the resources to keep his promise.

We live in a world system that makes grand and sweeping promises about what it can deliver in life. It promises us happiness, freedom, fulfillment, joy and contentment—if we will only live our lives the way the world system woos us to do. The problem is that, when we answer the siren call of our world system and live the way it calls us to live, we discover that it can't deliver on its promises. When all is said and done, we end up asking the same question as singer Peggy Lee: "Is that all there is?"

God speaks to us about this in the Bible. He says in Jeremiah 2:13, "My people . . . have forsaken Me, the fountain of living waters, to hew for themselves cisterns, broken cisterns that can hold no water." A cistern is a large tank for collecting and storing water. People used cisterns in biblical times, in places where there was no natural supply of water, to try and ensure that there would be a steady supply of drinking water.

Obviously, the best of all situations was to have a natural, clear-running spring. The next best thing was to have an unbroken cistern that collected and stored water effectively. The worst of all situations was to have a broken cistern that could not hold water. God declares that, when it comes to meeting the needs of our lives, he is a spring of living water (*mayim chayim* in Hebrew). Out of him springs all the happiness, freedom, fulfillment, joy and contentment we will ever need.

He also declares that what this world system offers us are broken cisterns that don't hold water. Power, money, fortune, fame, possessions, notoriety, partying, sexual activity—these are empty answers to empty promises.

As we conclude this chapter, I want to challenge you: don't live your life for broken cisterns that cannot hold water. Don't listen to the siren call of a world system making you empty promises. The Good Shepherd has so much more that he wants to give you. He wants to give you springs of living water, bubbling up and over in your soul, so that you can confidently say in all of life, "I shall not want."

In Psalm 125:1 David declares: "Those who trust in the LORD are as Mount Zion, which cannot be moved but abides forever." My friend, let me tell you where to plant your trust and devotion in life. You plant it in the Great Shepherd. You plant it 100 percent in the risen Lord Jesus. Let it dig deeply into him and it will hold you like nothing else will.

"The LORD is my shepherd, I shall not want." Make this the foundation for your life and you will not want. That's the promise of God, and God always keeps his promises!

Lord Jesus, I am your needy sheep and you are my all-sufficient shepherd. I thank you that, whatever I need, you have promised to supply. I thank you that this promise is without condition or exception. I thank you that this promise is backed up by your eternal and omnipotent power. I thank you that this promise held true for Abraham and Isaac and Jacob and Ruth and David— and for every sheep of God who has ever lived.

I pray that the example I see in their lives will comfort and motivate me to trust you with every ounce of my being. I pray it will reassure my heart in the tough times and rejuvenate my soul in the weary times. Thank you for carrying me when I am too feeble to carry myself. Thank you for seeking me when I wander off into perilous territory. Thank you for guiding me with your wisdom and for devising a perfect plan for me as an individual.

Lord, I ask you to continue to show mercy and tender grace to me as your ever-wandering sheep. In Jesus' name, I pray. Amen!

PART THREE

HE MAKES ME TO LIE DOWN IN GREEN PASTURES

**. . . He leads me beside the still waters.
He restores my soul.**

I cannot remember the first time that I ever heard the words of the 23rd Psalm. Maybe it was in the religious classes that I attended in the synagogue growing up as a young Jewish boy or perhaps in a synagogue service itself. As a child in the public education system of America in the 1950s and 1960s, I listened to a portion of the Bible read over the loudspeaker every morning, and so perhaps it was there that I first heard the psalm.

But even though I cannot remember where or when I first heard the psalm, I can remember what I thought for years about the words of verse 2: "He makes me to lie down in green pastures; He leads me beside the still waters." I thought this meant that God was promising me lots of great food to eat and water to drink. To a sheep, fresh green grass is as good as it gets. It's their meal of choice. Promising a sheep green grass is like promising a policeman hot Krispy Kreme donuts! To a sheep, sparkling clear water also ranks at the top of the list for beverages.

But when I studied this verse more closely, I discovered that this is not at all what God is talking about here. God does promise to meet all our material and dietary needs, it's true. But the promise God makes to his sheep in this verse has nothing to do with literal food or drink. The real meaning here has to do with our souls. In verse 2, God is promising us as his sheep that he will supply rich provisions, not just for our outward physical beings, but for our inner spiritual beings as well.

Let's look together at each of the phrases that make up this verse.

"He makes me to lie down in green pastures." The Hebrew word translated "pastures" doesn't mean pasture in the literal grazing sense. It has a broader meaning. It means "an attractive place that is full of rich green grass." Actually, a good translation of this word would be "verdant meadow." God is not promising us, his sheep, that he will let us eat our fill of grass in a field somewhere. Rather, God is promising that he will allow us to lie down and rest in lush green grassy meadows.

Now to understand this imagery, we need to think about what happens in the everyday life of a shepherd and his sheep. Every morning, the shepherd would lead his sheep out to pasture for the day. After they had eaten their fill for the morning, the sheep would then begin to chew their cud. The shepherd's job at that point was to find a restful, peaceful place of repose for the sheep to lie down during the heat of the day and properly digest their food. This is what the 23rd Psalm is talking about when it says, "He makes me to lie down in green pastures." The subject is not food at all. The subject is the refreshment, rest and rejuvenation that the shepherd knows his sheep need and that he makes sure his sheep get.

"He leads me beside the still waters." When translated literally from the original Hebrew, "still waters" mean "waters of security, waters of tranquility, waters of quiet rest." The focus here once again is on refreshment and serenity for one's inner soul, not on drinking water. When we carefully look at David's words, we realize that he said nothing about the sheep drinking this water. Instead, the picture here is that of the shepherd leading his sheep to a place of rest *next to* quiet, peaceful waters.

At McLean Bible Church in the Virginia suburbs of Washington, D.C., where I have served as the pastor for more than a quarter of a century, we recently completed the building of a new campus. As we worked with the architects and planners in designing the building complex, they kept encouraging us to have a water feature—a focal point where there was water running. The reason, they kept telling us, is because running water is the most soothing and calming element in the world of nature.

Now this is not true just for human beings. It's just as true for sheep. The reason the shepherd led his sheep to a place next to running water was because it was a location where the sheep could experience the highest level of serenity and tranquility.

"He restores my soul." Just in case someone missed the message that David was trying to convey by using the imagery of green pastures and still waters, he now comes right out and says what all this imagery is supposed to mean for us who are God's sheep. What all this means for us, says David, is that God promises to restore our soul as we face the daily struggles of life.

David wants us to understand that this verse has

nothing to do with God promising to meet the needs of our bodies. God is promising instead to meet the needs of our souls. Just as the shepherd makes sure he gets his sheep to a place where they can enjoy inner security, inner refreshment and inner recouping of strength, so God promises that he will personally minister to our hearts in such a way that we experience this same kind of inner rejuvenation and restoration of hope.

"Forget about shepherds and sheep for a minute," says David, "and let me give it to you straight. God restores my soul. He gives life and vitality to my innermost being. When my heart is discouraged, he revives it with hope. When my soul is weary, he strengthens it with supernatural stamina. When my soul is dry and withered, he waters it with the truth of his promises. When my heart is afraid, he reassures it. When my soul is lonely, he cheers it up with his personal presence. When my heart is overburdened with cares that I can't seem to bear, he comes to me and offers to carry the load for me. When I am fretting and consumed with worry and doubt, he tells me to give all my anxiety to him and he will replace it with the peace of God that passes all understanding. In short, God restores my soul."

This is the great promise of verse 2: whatever it takes to restore my soul, that's what my heavenly shepherd is committed to providing for me as his sheep. He wants my soul to be refreshed, spiritually satiated and at peace in every situation of life.

One of the greatest examples of this truth in action is found in the life of David himself. You may remember that David lived out in the Judean desert as a fugitive and a renegade for seven years as King Saul chased him around. Some of this time was spent on the western side of the Negev desert, where he used the little town of

Ziklag as the headquarters for his men and their families. In 1 Samuel 30, David and his men returned to Ziklag from a military foray, only to find that a band of marauding Amalekites had raided the city. Now watch what happens.

"Then it happened when David and his men came to Ziklag on the third day, that the Amalekites had . . . burned it with fire; and they took captive the women and all who were in it, both small and great, without killing anyone, and carried them off and went their way" (1 Samuel 30:1–2).

Now no one in their right mind wanted to be taken captive by the Amalekites. We know from the archaeological data that the Amalekites turned captive women into prostitutes and that they sold captive children as slaves to travelers along the caravan routes of the Middle East. This is why the Amalekites didn't kill any of the wives or children of David and his men.

When David and his men approached the city of Ziklag and saw what had happened, the Bible says, "David and the people who were with him lifted their voices and wept until there was no strength in them to weep" (1 Samuel 30:4). This is a powerful statement. To weep until there are no more tears left to cry is a level of grief that few of us ever experience. It takes a horrific tragedy to produce this in a person's life and that's exactly what had happened to David and his men.

In their anger, David's men turned on him. They began to talk of stoning him to death. So on top of the intense grief that David was feeling over the loss of his own family, he now had to deal with the fear and paranoia that comes from knowing that his men are about to mutiny and turn on him. David was clearly at his wit's end, totally strung out and empty.

I can't tell you how many times I have been right

where David was. In the early years, before my daughter
Jill's condition was adequately diagnosed and effective
treatment begun, she was in the hospital for days at a
time. The rescue squad became regular visitors at our
house because Jill would have seizures that we could not
stop without intravenous medication. Brenda and I
watched as Jill's life seemed to be ebbing away and no
matter what we tried, we were helpless to stop it. On top
of all this was the exhaustion factor. For years, Brenda
and I never slept through an entire night because Jill was
up having seizures in the middle of the night. The
cumulative effect of all this pain and exhaustion was that
Brenda and I became worn down until we reached the
point where David was in 1 Samuel 30: strung out and
empty in every part of our being. Depression became our
constant companion. Every time some new doctor or
some new medication gave us a glimmer of hope, it
would fail and our glimmer of hope would be painfully
dashed to the ground. I know full well what it means to
have a soul that desperately needs to be "restored." And
perhaps you do too.

Look what David did when he was in this depressed
state: "And David strengthened himself in the Lord his
God" (1 Samuel 30:6). His troops were going to stone him.
His family was gone. His men's wives and children were
gone. He had wept until he could weep no more. His city
was burned to the ground. All of his possessions were
destroyed. It was a total catastrophe. So what does David
do amid all this destruction and disaster? The Bible says
that he "strengthened himself in the Lord his God."

In other words, David turned to God with all his heart
and let God "restore his soul." He brought all his exigency
before God and allowed God to give him back perspective.
He let God give him back hope. He let God give him back

the courage he needed to be proactive in this disastrous situation. He let God give him back the calm and self-control he needed to respond to his situation biblically.

Because David let God restore his soul, he was able to seize the initiative and go to his men with a solution. He said to them, "Now, men, let's not act rashly here. Let's seek the Lord on this and find out what he wants us to do." As a result of David's calming influence, his men resorted to consulting God for wisdom rather than reacting in destructive anger. The outcome was that, in obedience to God's instructions, David and his men were able to follow the Amalekites' trail, ambush them and rescue their wives and children unharmed. Not only did David and his men get their wives and children back safely, but they also got all the treasures of the Amalekites for their own.

In short, God was able to take what looked like a total disaster and turn it into a great blessing. But this happened only because David understood this principle: that when everything else around us is falling apart, we have a Great Shepherd who is willing and anxious to restore our soul—to give new hope to our lives, to bring godly wisdom to our perspective on circumstances and to strengthen us to act biblically in our situation.

You know, I sometimes wonder if perhaps David wrote the 23rd Psalm after his experience at Ziklag. Or at least maybe the truths of verse 2 struck him after that crisis.

God wants to have a restoring ministry to our souls as his sheep. This is true, I believe, not just in mighty crises like David faced at Ziklag. Oh, we'll have these crises for sure and God will be there to restore our souls just like he promises. But here in Psalm 23, I believe David is talking about more than crises. I believe he's telling us that God wants to restore our souls in every situation of everyday life. Every day, God wants to bring us to the green meadows and the still waters that he has for our souls. Every day, God wants to minister refreshment and rejuvenation to our spirits. And if we'll let him, he will.

The good news is that God knows exactly how to restore a soul. I don't care where your soul is or what it's struggling with. I don't care how low your soul is feeling or how bad the problems are—God knows how to restore your soul. He's been doing it for thousands of years. He's done it for people with problems far worse than yours. He can handle the needs of your soul if you'll let him.

Now there are a couple of corollaries I'd like to add.

Number one—How does God restore a soul? We saw that David strengthened himself in the Lord, but honestly, exactly what does that mean and how do we do it as God's sheep in the 21st century? I offer you two suggestions.

First, God uses the promises of the Bible to restore a soul. This explains why Psalm 19:7 says, "The law of the LORD is perfect, *restoring the soul.*" How often when we're discouraged and depleted does God use a word, a verse or a promise from the Bible to lift us up and give us some encouragement? I love what Paul says in Colossians 3:15–16: "Let the peace of Christ rule in your hearts," and he goes on to explain that one way to do that is to "Let the word of Christ richly dwell within you." This is what the hymn writer had in mind when he said, "Standing on the promises of Christ my King."[3] This is one of the strategic ways in which God restores a soul: he brings the promises of God to bear on our problems and, suddenly, fortified by the promises that the God who cannot lie has made to us, we find a new perspective and a new sense of hope entering into our lives.

During those times of intense pain and struggle with

my daughter's situation, God used a verse I mentioned earlier, Jeremiah 29:11, to restore my soul again and again: "'For I know the plans that I have for you,' declares the LORD, 'plans for welfare and not for calamity to give you a future and a hope.'" During those moments, when it seemed like my world was coming apart at the seams and that all hope was gone on the human level, I would reflect on this great verse where God promises me that my pain and anguish are not a random happening. Rather, they are all part of God's sovereign and inscrutable plan for my life, a plan designed for my good and benefit. As I would embrace this promise in faith, believing it even though I couldn't see how all the pieces fit together quite yet, a new sense of hope and resilience would return to my soul. In other words, God used his promise in Jeremiah 29:11 to "restore my soul."

As God's sheep, when we need to have our souls restored, one of the first places we need to go is into the Bible to remind ourselves of God's promises. The reason for this is simple: God has designed and given his promises to us for the purpose of restoring our souls on the daily treadmill of life.

Second, God restores people's souls through the supernatural ministry of the Holy Spirit directly to our hearts. God has the ability to come into a soul and to supernaturally minister encouragement, comfort, peace, serenity and rejuvenation. This is simply the personal ministry of God's Spirit in the life of his sheep. I can't explain to you exactly how the Spirit does this because, frankly, I don't *know* how he does it. But I know that he does it!

Remember that this is what Jesus himself said to us when he was here on earth. He said, "My peace I leave with you. My peace I give you" (John 14:27 NKJV) When we fall on our knees before God and cry out to him with souls that are heavy with pain and discouragement, God responds. By the working of his Spirit directly upon our hearts, God lifts our load and brightens our step. It's not that the situations of life have changed. Rather, it's that God has restored our souls in spite of the situation. And as I said earlier, I don't understand nor can I (or anyone else) explain exactly how the Spirit performs this ministry to our souls. But then, God doesn't ask us to understand or explain it—just to yield to him and allow him to do it for us.

This is what the hymn writer meant when he wrote: "There is a place of quiet rest . . . a place of comfort sweet . . . a place where we our Savior meet . . . a place of full release . . . a place where all is joy and peace, near to the heart of God."⁴ When we, in humble surrender and prayer, bring to God all our anxiety, all our care, all our pain and grief and confusion and exhaustion—and we give it all to him—then supernaturally, by the power of the Spirit, God restores our soul at that place. And in the daily struggles of life, this is a place that we need to visit often.

Number two—We need to realize that God never gets tired of restoring souls. This is an awesome truth to realize. Frankly, as a pastor, I get tired sometimes. I get tired of the telephone ringing and people calling and saying that they have problems and need my help. I get tired of people wanting to talk to me and tell me about their pain and heartache. Sometimes I feel like saying to people, "You know, I'm sorry, but no, we can't talk now, because frankly, I've got nothing left to give."

Now, be honest, if you were in distress and pain and you went to your spiritual leader and he dismissed you like that, it would really bother you—true?

Well, the good news is that God *never* does this. When we as his sheep come to him in need of a restoration of our soul, we never meet with *anything* but a receptive embrace from our heavenly shepherd. No matter how many times we have fallen; no matter how many times we keep getting discouraged; no matter how many times we come to God with our souls in need of restoring—God never says: "Oh no, not her again! Oh no, I can't believe he's back so soon!"

When I was growing up, I loved to watch the western serial *The Lone Ranger* on TV. And you know what? Every week, in every crisis, without fail, the Lone Ranger would come to the rescue of the person in need. He never got tired. I never once heard the Lone Ranger say to Tonto, "Why don't they go ask somebody else for help? I'm sick of people always coming to me." Would the Lone Ranger say that? Of course not.

Now God is just like the Lone Ranger, only better, because he's real. God never begrudges helping his sheep. He never gets tired of restoring our souls. He never says "no" or "I'm out of resources" or "I've got nothing left to give." As the great hymn says, "For out of His infinite riches in Jesus, he giveth, and giveth, and giveth again."[5]

What's the point? Well, don't ever let anyone convince you that you've come to God too many times to restore your soul. God doesn't have a quota system when it comes to restoring souls. We can come to God every hour of every day of every week of every month of every year for the rest of our lives to get our souls restored— and God is tickled pink! He never gets weary of restoring your soul and he never will. So approach him with confidence and boldness.

Number three and finally—God is the only one who can do this kind of restoring of people's souls. Please notice carefully the pronoun that David uses here in Psalm 23: "HE makes me to lie down in green pastures. HE leads me beside the still waters. HE restores my soul." David makes it clear that there is only one place where people can get this kind of soul-restoring ministry—and that is from the heavenly shepherd.

People can cheer us up. People can make us laugh. People can put an arm around us and try to console us. People can pray with us and for us. People can give us money and bring us meals and take us to the doctor. But people cannot restore our souls.

The arts can excite us. Music can give us some fulfillment. Physical activity can give us some release. Hobbies can occupy our time. Community involvement can make us feel like we're making a positive contribution to our world. Parties and alcohol and drugs and sex can give us a temporary thrill. But none of these things can restore our souls.

Only Jesus can restore and satisfy our souls. There really are green pastures and still waters for our souls. These are places where Jesus really does lead *his* sheep. And what's more—there is no crisis or tragedy so dark that the Lord can't restore a soul in the midst of it. So don't waste time looking to the world system to do for you what only Jesus can do.

There are people in the church where I pastor who have been through some of life's darkest hours. And they will tell you that when the hour was the darkest, Jesus shone the brightest. They will tell you that even at the bottom of the "black hole" God is quite capable of restoring souls, because he did it for them.

Maybe some of us have never been to such places in our lives, but we know people who have been there and we need to accept their testimony—and the statement of God himself—that there is no sorrow that is beyond the reach of God's supernatural, soul-restoring power.

If you were to ask the average follower of Christ to list his or her top-ten favorite hymns, one hymn would appear on virtually every list. It is the hymn "It Is Well with My Soul."

Horatio G. Spafford, a Chicago businessman, wrote this powerful hymn at a time of great tragedy and anguish in his life. Two years after his business burned down in the great Chicago fire of 1871, Mr. Spafford decided to take his wife and four daughters for a vacation in England. He had originally planned to travel together with his family across the Atlantic, but a last minute business meeting detained him. So he sent his wife and four girls on ahead with the promise that he would follow them in a day or two. As their ship crossed the North Atlantic on a dark and stormy night, another vessel rammed into it. The stricken ship sank in only twelve minutes. As his wife clung to a piece of wreckage, she watched as all four of her daughters were swept away and drowned. She was rescued and taken to Wales, where she cabled back to Mr. Spafford two words: "Saved alone."

When he received the telegram, Mr. Spafford immediately booked passage on a ship following the same route to England as the ship his family had taken. He asked the captain to please inform him when the ship reached the spot where his daughters had drowned, be it day or night. About 2 A.M. one morning, the cabin steward knocked on his door and informed Mr. Spafford that in fifteen minutes they would be at "his spot." Mr. Spafford dressed and went up on deck. He stood on the bow under the dim lights of the bridge as the ship passed over the watery grave of his four little girls.

Mr. Spafford had not planned on writing anything. But as God began restoring his soul, as he stood there knowing that his four daughters' bodies were under that water somewhere, he took out an old envelope and pencil that he discovered in his coat pocket, and he began to write down his thoughts. He wrote:

> When peace, like a river, attendeth my way,
> When sorrows like sea billows roll;
> Whatever my lot, Thou hast taught me to say
> It is well, it is well, with my soul.

Did you ever wonder why the first verse of this hymn is full of sea-faring imagery? Well, now you know.

> Though Satan should buffet, though trials should come,
> Let this blest assurance control,
> That Christ has regarded my helpless estate,
> And hath shed His own blood for my soul.
> My sin, oh, the bliss of this glorious thought!
> My sin, not in part but the whole
> Is nailed to the cross, and I bear it no more,
> Praise the Lord, praise the Lord, O my soul!

> And Lord, haste the day when my faith shall be sight,
> The clouds be rolled back as a scroll;
> The trump shall resound, and the Lord shall descend,
> Even so, it is well with my soul.[6]

Friends, this hymn has been a source of hope, comfort and encouragement for literally thousands of Christ-followers for almost 150 years. I seldom officiate at a funeral where it isn't sung or performed. But (and this is the key point) this hymn would never have been written—and it would never have been around to strengthen the souls of thousands of people—if its author had not allowed God to restore his soul even in its darkest hour. This is why I believe "It Is Well with My Soul" has such a powerful effect upon people in tragedy and loss—because it came out of a man who experienced deep tragedy and loss, but a man who also knew how to turn to Jesus to get his soul restored.

I trust, my dear friends, when you find yourself in pain and anguish of soul, like Horatio Spafford did, that you will remember this story and let God do for you what he did for Spafford. I hope that you will always be able to say "Whatever my lot, it is well with my soul"—not because things always go well but because God keeps restoring your soul in spite of how things go.

"He makes me to lie down in green pastures. He leads me beside the still waters. He restores my soul." Where would we go—what would we do—if we didn't have a God who restored the soul? But we do have such a heavenly shepherd! And we thank him for it.

Lord Jesus, I thank you that, in the darkest hours of life, you are there to restore my soul. And not just in life's darkest hours is this true but in every hour of life. I am so grateful that you are a God who can reach into the deepest recesses of my soul and do a work of renewal there that no one else can do. Lord, teach me to turn to no other source for restoration of soul than you. Remind me that all other sources of spiritual encouragement and renewal are vain. They are broken cisterns, while you are the living fountain of living water.

Forgive me, Lord, for trying to find in other places what can only be found in you. May I learn to make you my exclusive place of refuge and strength, now and forevermore. In Jesus' name, Amen.

PART FOUR

HE LEADS ME IN THE PATHS OF RIGHTEOUSNESS

. . . for His Name's sake.

We come now to the second amplifying promise that God gives to his sheep—divine guidance. This promise can be broken down into three key parts. First, *what* God does—"He leads me." Second, *where* God does this—"in the paths of righteousness." And third, *why* he does it—"for his name's sake."

First, let's talk about *what* God does. The Bible says, "He leads me."

In ancient Israel, shepherds spent their entire lives leading and guiding their sheep. There's a reason for this. Put simply, sheep are utterly incapable of leading themselves. Sheep have neither the self-determination nor the situational awareness to get through life on their own. Sheep need to have constant care and guidance from their shepherd.

What's more, sheep have notoriously poor eyesight. Basically, they can only see what is right in front of their noses. To make matters worse, sheep are not capable of thinking strategically. It is not part of a sheep's DNA to look out on the horizon, scrutinize the landscape in front of him and then make and execute a plan to weave his way where he needs to go. He just can't do it.

Apart from the guiding influence of their shepherd, sheep will simply remain in the same place and graze until they've gnawed the vegetation down to the roots. Next, rather than moving along on their own, they'll actually tear the roots right out of the ground. Finally, if left to themselves, sheep will actually starve to death in the very pastures they've destroyed!

Therefore, one of the major jobs of a good shepherd is to guide his sheep every day. He does this by walking in front of them—"leading them," if you will. In John 10:4, Jesus refers to this practice when he says that the good shepherd goes before his sheep and they follow him, for they know his voice. The job descriptions here are quite simple: the shepherd leads and the sheep follow. When the shepherd turns left, the sheep turn left. When the shepherd turns right, the sheep turn right. When he goes straight, they go straight. When he stops, they stop. This is why it's such a serious thing to be a shepherd, because wherever you lead your sheep, they *will* follow you. If you lead them into danger, they'll follow you. If you lead them to bad pastures, they'll follow you. If you lead them right over a cliff, they'll follow you.

I am confident that it was this imagery that Jesus had in mind—and that every person in ancient Israel would have understood instinctively—when he said of some of the Jewish religious leaders of his day, "They are blind guides of the blind. And if a blind man guides a blind man, both will fall into a pit" (Matthew 15:14). As a shepherd, David appreciated this truth in a way that even the average Israelite did not. He had spent years leading his father's sheep around in the Judean wilderness. He realized that if he hadn't been there to do this for his sheep, they would have been helpless to survive and prosper on their own.

That's why I believe that, one day, as he was reflecting on how tenderly and faithfully God had guided his life, David suddenly made the connection and said to himself: "Wow! You know what? Just like a good shepherd, God understands how nearsighted I am as his sheep. Just like a good shepherd, God realizes that on my own, I cannot strategically plan my way through the complex mazes of life. Just like a good shepherd, God knows that he's got to get personally involved in leading me or I'm going to fall into some ditch somewhere. And, Lord, because you understand how helpless I am, and because you are the Good Shepherd, you have committed yourself totally to guiding my life. You didn't have to do this, but in your love and compassion for me as your sheep, you voluntarily decided to do it. And I thank you for it."

Now there is a very popular theological fad around today that goes like this: God doesn't treat us like babies. God doesn't want to run every part of our lives. God wants us to choose our own paths in life. So God simply sets up the big parameters—the "big fences"—around my field as his sheep. We know these as the black-and-white commandments of the Bible. As long as I don't transgress these big black-and-white commands, God has little interest in the smaller choices I make—my career, my mate, the college I attend, the house I buy, the car I purchase, the business decisions I make, the choices of my daily routine. As long as I stay inside the big fences, basically any choice I make about these things is fine with God. He doesn't really involve himself at this level of my daily activities.

I want to say that, in my opinion, this kind of teaching is absolutely wrong. What's worse, it threatens to rob us of one of the most precious and valuable benefits that Almighty God offers us as his sheep—namely, his offer to lead and guide us personally.

However, the proponents of this distorted "big fence" theory are correct about one thing: God doesn't treat us like babies. Instead, God treats us like *sheep*! And whether it insults our selfish pride or not, the truth is that sheep need leading. They always have and they always will.

The Good Shepherd offers to walk in front of us and guide our choices through the maze of life—because, as sheep, we need him to. We don't have to figure out all of life's permutations or understand how to make the choices that will maximize our purpose in life and bring richness to our souls—because, as sheep, we can't. God offers to do all that for us, using his vastly superior wisdom and foreknowledge. Our job is simply to relax and to follow his directions, knowing that every choice into which he leads us will, by definition, be one that brings blessing and fulfillment to our lives.

In order for us to follow the Good Shepherd effectively and let him guide us through the endless possibilities that life offers, we must first realize that this option exists. When some well-meaning theologian convinces us that it doesn't—that God isn't really interested in the individual details and everyday choices of life—we will stop looking to God for his everyday guidance. We will, by our own actions, rob ourselves of one of the greatest and most precious services God offers us.

The Bible is literally bursting with examples and promises about God leading his people at the everyday detail level of life. Remember, for example, the Israelites in the Sinai wilderness after their exodus from Egypt. The Bible tells us that God sent a cloud and a pillar of fire to guide them on a daily and hourly basis. The Bible says that when God lifted the cloud, it was a sign to the Israelites that he wanted them to break camp and follow that cloud to the next destination that the Lord sovereignly had chosen for them. Wherever the cloud stopped, that's where the Israelites would camp until the Lord repeated the process.

What clearer example could God show us when it comes to how he wants to lead his people? The people of Israel followed God's cloud step-by-step, moment by moment, day by day for 40 years in the wilderness. God gave those people specific, detailed, down-to-the-smallest-iota guidance. What we have here is a simple case of the shepherd leading and the sheep following. And the Bible tells us that this arrangement worked out well for everybody. The Israelites never lacked food to eat, water to drink or protection from their enemies in their 40 years of wandering in the harsh and inhospitable Sinai.

Then there's the story of Abraham sending his servant to look for a wife for his son, Isaac. The Bible records that Abraham's servant prayed as he went and asked God to lead him precisely to the perfect woman for his master's son. He describes his reaction when he found Rebecca: "I bowed low and worshiped the LORD, and blessed the LORD, the God of my master Abraham, who had guided me in the right way to take the daughter of my master's kinsman for his son" (Genesis 24:48).

Abraham's servant believed that, if he relied on God to do so, God would lead him to the *exact* woman God had chosen for Isaac. He believed that God actually cared about such everyday choices such as whom Isaac would marry, and that God was willing to take a personal interest in helping the choice turn out well, if the servant would simply rely on God to do so.

Where did this servant get such a perspective on God's leading? I believe the answer is clear: he got it from his master. Abraham believed that God was anxious and willing to lead his people in life's everyday affairs, because he had seen God do this very thing for him ever since God had called him to leave Ur in Genesis 12.

Let's add to these examples some actual promises that God has made about his willingness to lead our lives on an everyday detail basis.

> **Psalm 32:8:** "I will instruct you and teach you in the way which you should go. I will counsel you with My eye upon you."
> **Isaiah 30:21:** "Your ears will hear a word behind you, 'This is the way, walk in it,' whenever you turn to the right or to the left."
> **Isaiah 58:11:** "And the LORD will continually guide you."
> **Proverbs 3:5–6:** " Trust in the LORD with all your heart and do not lean on your own understanding. In all your ways acknowledge Him, and He will make your paths straight."
> **Proverbs 16:9:** "The mind of man plans his way, but the LORD directs his steps."

Look at all this assurance that God gives regarding his offer to guide our choices in life and to lead us like a shepherd. This is why David prayed, "O LORD, lead me in Your righteousness . . . Make Your way straight before me" (Psalm 5:8).

The bottom line here, my friend, is that Almighty God *wants* to lead your life. He's aching to lead your life. He's not aching to lead your life in just the big things. God wants to lead your life down to the smallest, most intimate details. For us to reject this offer and refuse this kind of guidance is crazy. But in order to appropriate it, we've first got to believe God is willing to do it. God wants you to believe this. That's why he prompted David to write in the 23rd Psalm, "He leads me."

I pray about parking spaces—do you? When I drive into Washington, D.C., I pray, "Now, Lord, you know I need to park somewhere. I know you can go before me and guide me to a place where the right car will be pulling out of the right spot at just the right time for my arrival. And I'm asking you to please do that for me." I pray the same way when I go to the mall at Christmastime. You say, "Does this really work?" Well, all I can tell you is that I find some of the most unbelievable parking spaces!

When I go out to buy a house, which isn't that often, but when I do, I pray for God's direct leading. I believe that God has a specific house to which he will lead me and in which he will bless me if I'll trust him to do so.

When I buy a car, it's the same way. I pray about which school I should send my children to. And, oh brother, did I pray about my marriage partner! I believe that one of the reasons I got one of the greatest wives in the world is because for years I prayed for God to guide me *specifically* to just the right woman.

In my family, we have just worked our way through this great truth in the life of my youngest son, Jonathan. Since he was a little boy, Jonathan's dream has been to play college (and maybe professional) baseball. Through all the years of Little League, Babe Ruth baseball and high school baseball, Jon has never relinquished his dream. So as we approached the end of his junior year in high school, the college recruiting process suddenly gobbled us up.

Having never done this before, we were all a little overwhelmed by the dissonance and the roller-coaster nature of the process. It has no real symmetry or order to it. Coaches call and write you. They invite you to showcase camps. They ask you to fill out recruitment forms. Then you wait and wonder. Some weeks you feel you're their first choice and then, without warning, you seem to have slipped into oblivion. The entire process creates a huge sense of insecurity and uncertainty.

Going through this together with my son, I realized that God had created a real teaching opportunity. So I tried to grab it. Of course, I had no idea how this was all going to turn out—where Jon would finally end up playing college baseball or even *if* he would. But I knew that God could be trusted to lead Jon perfectly through this maze. I adopted a mantra that I kept sharing with Jon. I would say, "Jon, God already has it worked out. All we have to do is let him lead and then follow."

I'd amplify: "Jon, God's got a college already picked out where the will of God for you runs through that school. And if we'll just trust him, he'll see to it that you end up there. We don't need to try and figure it all out or control it. We just need to watch as God opens and shuts doors in his own divine providence—and then just keep walking through the doors God opens. As this recruiting process goes up and down and all around, Jon, let's just reaffirm every day our confidence that God's going to lead you perfectly through this morass. Let's not fret, let's trust."

Well, just as I knew he would, God led Jon to a good and blessed conclusion—to a top-fifteen university that has an impressive baseball program and where the coach really is high on him. It's the best of both worlds: the chance to play college baseball and attend a prestigious educational institution.

And as we were talking recently, Jon said to me: "You know, as I look back now, I can see how God was leading the whole time. I know that this is exactly where God has chosen for me to go."

I replied, "Jon, you're absolutely right. Now, in the years to come, allow this experience to color your approach to all of life. Don't forget what the Lord has shown you here. He has a perfect plan for you, down to the smallest details of life. And if you'll let him, he'll guide you into it, no matter how confusing it may look at first glance."

Friends, God has a will—God has a plan—for every one of our lives as his sheep. He has chosen a pathway for every part of *your* life, down to the littlest things. It's a plan that will bring you the greatest fulfillment and blessing possible. It's a pathway you could never discover or figure out on your own.

This is why I don't *want* to choose my own path in life. I don't want God to put me in a big field with just a few big fences and say to me, "OK, Lon, just pick whatever you want to pick." I don't have the wisdom for this kind of setup. I insisted on this kind of arrangement with God for a number of years and got myself into more trouble than you could shake a stick at. I'm a sheep who needs guidance every day—and I know it!

Therefore, I want God to show me everything, down to the smallest details of life. I want him to be intimately involved in all the choices I make. And the great news of Psalm 23 is that God is happy to do this for me, if I'll just let him.

This is God's promise: "He leads me" as his sheep. I

believe this totally. And I want you to believe it too. I don't want anybody to convince you differently. God cares about every detail of your life and he'll guide your choices in those details, if you'll let him.

Hymn writer Sidney Cox wrote, "My Lord knows the way through the wilderness. All I have to do is follow."[7] This is the division of labor that leads to maximum blessing in life.

Next, let's look at *where* God leads us. David says that God leads us "in the paths of righteousness."

The Good Shepherd never leads his sheep down harmful paths. He leads them on paths that bring blessing, prosperity and fulfillment. God knows that these things only come from living a certain way. That's why David says that God leads us in the paths of righteousness. Regardless of his individual plan for his sheep, God leads every sheep down the path of holy, righteous, virtuous living.

Lest there be any misunderstanding, I want to say categorically that God has laid out in the Bible his definition of righteous and virtuous living. To say that God leads us in the paths of righteousness is merely to say that God always leads us in paths of biblical obedience. If you only knew the people I've had come into my office over the years and try to convince me that God had led them some other way. I've had people sit there and try to tell me that God led them to falsify documents, to lie to customers about the product they were selling, to have an adulterous affair, to shack up before marriage, to break the civil law, to cheat and lie and deceive in every imaginable way. I've had people sit in my office and try to convince me that God led them to break promises they made, renege on commitments they gave, violate legal contracts they signed, take revenge on other people and refuse to forgive others who had hurt them.

And I've had to say to every one of these folks, "I don't know who led you to do these things, but I can assure you it was **not** God. God never leads anybody anywhere but down the paths of righteousness, and that means God never leads anyone anywhere but in obedience to the principles and commands of the Bible." Now, we know who really led all these people in my office, don't we? Of course we do. They led themselves! They led themselves into doing things that they felt like doing and then they blamed it on God—especially when their choices led to trouble.

God gets credit for a lot of "leading" that he never does. One of the ways we can verify whether it's truly God who is leading us to make some choice in life is to ask the question, "Does this course of action square with the clear teachings of the Bible?" If not, I can assure you, without reservation, it is not God who is leading us to make that choice. If someone or something is leading you down a path of biblical disobedience—or even if you're trying to justify leading yourself there—be forewarned. You need to reject that course of action as one that will ultimately lead to heartache and regret. God never, ever leads people down these paths. God only leads down the paths of righteousness, which means he only leads according to the ways that he defines in the Bible as honorable and virtuous.

Finally, let's look at *why* God leads like this. David says that God leads like this "for His name's sake."

Yes, it's true that God leads us down the paths of righteousness for our sake—for our blessing and happiness. But there's an even bigger reason why God leads this way. God leads us as his people down the paths of righteousness for the sake of his own reputation.

When David committed adultery and impregnated
Bathsheba, the wife of one of his faithful soldiers, and
then murdered that soldier in premeditated fashion, the
prophet Nathan came to visit him. Nathan told David a
little story about a rich man who took another man's only
sheep and killed it for food instead of the rich man using
one of the many sheep he owned. David was outraged
when he heard this and he demanded to know who the
perpetrator was so that he might be punished. Nathan
then said to David, "You are the man!" When David
heard this, he was devastated and cried out, "I have
sinned against the LORD" (2 Samuel 12:13).

Nathan's words in response are quite germane to our
topic here. Nathan said, "The LORD also has taken away
your sin; you shall not die. However . . . by this deed
you have given occasion to the enemies of the LORD to
blaspheme" (2 Samuel 12:13–14). Nathan tells David that
his heinous actions have created an opportunity for
God's enemies to speak evil of him, to impugn God's
character and sully his reputation. Because of this,
Nathan continues, "the child also that is born to you shall
surely die" (2 Samuel 12:14).

You see, David had created the most powerful empire
in the ancient Near East of his day. He had defeated the
kings of the Moabites, Edomites, Philistines, Syrians,
Phoenicians, Ammonites and many others. He had
proclaimed to them that he represented a righteous, holy
God who was the one and only true God of this world.
He had condemned their idolatrous gods as being
unholy, unrighteous and polluted. But now that David
had committed such a dastardly act, one that many of
these pagan kings themselves would not have done, he
had compromised the integrity and reputation of the
Holy One of Israel. Suddenly David had given cause for

all these other peoples to dismiss the true and living God as a joke. Nathan says to David, "Don't you understand what you have done? It's far more serious than adultery. It's even more serious than first-degree murder. You have given all these unbelieving pagans a chance to dismiss God as a travesty and to ridicule him."

This same reality exists in the world of shepherds and sheep. If we were to see a herd of sheep that looked emaciated, scrawny and haggard, we wouldn't judge the sheep. We'd immediately judge the shepherd. We'd think, "What an awful shepherd they must have." This is true of us as God's sheep. When our behavior, attitude and speech are ungodly and dishonorable, people around us don't stop their judgments at us. They also go on to judge our shepherd. Then they use these judgments to justify their unbelief.

This is a strategic truth for us to understand. Those of us who name the name of Christ as the one we follow become inextricably connected with his reputation and character in the eyes of an onlooking world. Our behavior and God's reputation become "joined at the hip" for life.

Anyone who's done much reaching out to people to try and bring them to faith in Jesus Christ has no doubt encountered this. Someone will quickly throw back in our face the objection that "I once knew a person who claimed to be a Christian and they did this and that unrighteous thing. How can I believe in this righteous God and perfect Savior you're talking about after they did what they did? Yada, yada, yada!" I believe that, a lot of the time, these people are telling us the truth about how they feel. I believe that for many in our world, the most serious roadblock between that person and a decision for Christ in their life is the inauthentic,

unrighteous behavior that they saw or experienced on
the part of some professing follower of Christ.

What this means is that there's a lot riding on how we
let God lead us. If we allow him to lead us in righteous
paths, where we exhibit biblically obedient behavior, we
ensure not only our own blessing but also God's
untarnished reputation. If we follow other paths, we
compromise both our blessing and God's reputation.

You know, there's an old saying, "You can lead a
horse to water but you can't make him drink." The same
is true of us and the leading of the Good Shepherd. God
can lead us in the paths of righteousness. He can offer to
direct our paths. But he can't make us follow. In the final
analysis, a sheep's got to want to follow his shepherd.

If you're like me, you may be thinking, "Honestly, I
really do want to follow God's leading. But sometimes
it's hard to do." Well, the good news is that God knows
our heart. If we are indeed sincere about following God,
then we will always find God to be compassionate and
patient with us. If we're weak but we want to follow,
God will provide us with the strength. If we're under
attack but we want to follow, God will intervene and
help us. If we always seem to be falling down and
failing, but we really want to follow, God will keep
picking us up and forgiving us.

I know this for a fact because it's the story of my life.
Since I gave my life to Jesus in early 1971, it has been
my most sincere and genuine desire to let God rule and
guide my life. And yet I've failed and fallen short too
many times to count. What I've discovered is that the
Lord has been infinitely patient and forgiving with me.
More times than I care to remember, God has picked me
up, dusted me off and preserved my life out of sheer
mercy—nothing else.

And all of this has taught me a most strategic truth: God cares most about intent, not performance. In other words, if the true intent of my heart is to follow God and obey his leading, then even if my actual performance sometimes falls short, God will still honor my heart's intent. He'll overrule my mistakes and overcome my shortcomings and forgive my frailties. And this too will be evident to those we look to bring to faith in our God.

So it's really a win-win situation. I get blessing and fulfillment when I follow. I find compassion and mercy when I fall short. And it's all because of the wonderful character of the Good Shepherd who adopted me as one of his sheep.

Dear Father, we are overwhelmed by your offer to guide our lives personally, intimately and down to life's smallest details. As sheep, we desperately need such guidance. But, as God, you are under no obligation to provide it. Yet you graciously reach out to us like a shepherd does to his sheep. You graciously extend to us both your hand and your heart. You do not leave us to wander aimlessly on our own, but you graciously walk ahead of us and invite us to follow, both for our benefit and for your glory.

Lord Jesus, give me the wisdom to admit my incapacity. Give me the wisdom to acknowledge my puny human understanding of life. Give me the wisdom to run to you as my Great Shepherd and to follow you gladly as you offer to direct the affairs of my life.

Lord, please forgive me for the many times that I stray from you and suddenly find myself in some dangerous and barren field. Thank you for your constant ministry of forgiveness and restoration back into the fold. Please create in me a steadfast heart—one that yearns to walk

right behind you as you direct my paths. Please help me
(by the Spirit's enabling power) to live out that yearning
faithfully and obediently every moment of every day.
And please be merciful and compassionate to me when I
fall short.

Prone to wander, Lord I feel it;
Prone to leave the God I love.
Here's my heart, O take and seal it,
Seal it for Thy courts above.[8]

Amen!

PART FIVE

YEA, THOUGH I WALK THROUGH THE VALLEY

**. . . of the shadow of death, I will fear no evil;
For You are with me;
Your rod and Your staff,
they comfort me.**

When I was a small child, I used to lie in bed motionless at night.

My bedroom was completely dark. Every time I'd hear a creak or a noise, I would open my eyes in fear, sure that there was going to be some horrible creature slinking around in my room.

I always fell asleep staring at my closet because I wanted to make sure if something awful popped out of there, I had maximum time to get out of the room. I was careful to never allow my arm or leg to hang out of the bed or even to be close to the edge. I always slept with my arms wrapped around my pillow under me, for I was sure there was some demonic being just waiting to reach up from under my bed and grab me.

I had nightmares of being pulled beneath my bed only to find that there was a secret doorway there that led to the inner recesses of hell. I had watched *The Twilight Zone* and I knew that this was exactly how these monsters grabbed kids and carried them off, never to be heard from again. I might mention that I still sleep in this pillow-hugging position to this day, uncomfortable when any part of me is hanging out of the bed, because you just never know what's under the bed!

I was terrified of going to bed every night. Fear literally gripped my life beginning about an hour before bedtime. While the lights were all on, I'd conduct a security search of my entire bedroom, but that still didn't solve the problem, because these creatures were able to slide in at any moment and I knew it. The worst moment of every day came when my dad would flip the light off and leave me alone in bed. The reason I made him flip off the light was because running from the light switch to the bed myself left me too exposed to being grabbed by some hellish being and whisked away forever.

Now, at this point, you might be thinking, "Lon, I sure hope you have a good therapist!"

But really, going back to my childhood, let me tell you how my father dealt with my fear. He would say to me, "Son, I'll be right in the next room. If anything tries to hurt you, give a call and I'll be right there." This really did help a lot. I'd lie there in bed and think to myself, "Now if some green, hairy, one-eyed, slobbering monster comes out of the closet, I'm going to call my dad and he'll come in here and take care of it." Somehow, the idea of my dad coming in to help was all I needed to hear. Sometimes, as I lay in bed awake, just to be sure, I'd yell out, "Hey, Dad, are you still out there?" And he'd send back that reassuring reply, "Yes I am, son, now relax and go to sleep. You're safe."

You see, here's the point: It was the presence of my father that made all the difference in how I faced the shadows and terrors of my bedroom.

Life is funny. Thirty years later, I found myself living out this same scenario, except that the roles had switched. Suddenly, when I turned off the light at night, I found my children saying, "Dad, where are you going to be?" They wanted to know exactly where I was and I knew why. They were afraid that some green, hairy, one-eyed, slobbering monster was going to grab them, and my presence as their dad brought calm and security to their hearts.

Every one of us knows what it's like to be afraid. Fear is a feeling that every human being has experienced. Sometimes fears are not genuine. Sometimes they're imaginary like mine were as a little boy. But even though there may be no basis in fact for our fears, the terror they generate is still quite real.

But then there are those times when our fear is justified because the danger is true. Maybe it's a time when we're facing financial ruin, or the possibility of terminal illness or we're doing poorly in school. Maybe we're in danger of losing our job, or our parents are talking about a divorce or we're pregnant and there's trouble with some of the initial tests on the baby. Maybe our car is making funny noises and we don't have any money to fix it or buy another one.

Whether our fears are real or imaginary, the solution God offers us is exactly the same. He doesn't offer us a solution that removes the danger, whether real or imaginary. God instead offers us the same solution my dad offered me and I in turn offered my children. He offers us the assurance of his personal presence. You see, when you're a sheep, the solution for fear is not the absence of danger but the presence of the shepherd.

This is what Psalm 23:4 is all about. "Yea, though I walk through the valley of the shadow of death, I will fear no evil; for You *are* with me."

This verse has given strength to many a follower of Christ going through crisis. It has restored hope to many a person facing tough times. It has comforted untold numbers of military men and women going into harm's way. It's probably one of the most beloved verses in the entire Bible. But this is more than just a beloved piece of biblical poetry. It is a verse that is packed with practical truth for our everyday lives as God's sheep. So let's take a look at it.

David begins by saying, "Yea, though I walk through the valley of the shadow of death, I will fear no evil."

In ancient Israel, shepherds would spend the winter in special quarters where the shepherd would sleep in a nice little tent and the sheep would be confined to a barnyard where they would be fenced in and fed. But in the spring, a shepherd would take his sheep out of their winter quarters and head up into the high country, where the winter rains had brought vegetation to the hillsides.

When the shepherd decided to move his flock from field to field during the summer, he always moved by way of the valleys, called "wadis" today. It was too hard to move a flock of sheep over the hills. Shepherds used the valleys because they had the gentlest grades and the smoothest roads. These paths also had the best food and plenty of water. But the valleys also held the greatest dangers for the sheep. There were natural disasters such as storms, mud slides, rock slides, hail. Perhaps most dangerous of all these natural dangers were the flash floods that would sweep through the wadis.

I have been leading tours to Israel for over twenty years and I have been in the country to see some of these

powerful flash floods. They occur after a heavy rainfall up
in the mountains around Jerusalem when the water runs
down toward the Dead Sea. In moments, a completely
dry wadi can become a rushing torrent, carrying away
everything in its path with devastating force. This can
include cars, buses and even military vehicles. And the
most dangerous part of these floods is that they strike
with absolutely no warning. Normally, the rainfall that
causes them is happening miles away, unseen and
unheard by the victim who is walking in the wadi. Should
a flock of sheep be in a wadi when one of these floods
comes through, not one of them would survive.

But natural disasters are not the only danger that
sheep faced in the valleys. They also faced the prospect
of predatory animals that would hide in the crevices and
pounce on the sheep as they passed by. The Bible
testifies to the presence of a number of these animals in
ancient Israel, including lions, bears and bobcats.

There were also robbers who would lie in wait to kill
the shepherd and steal the sheep.

In fact, the area between Jerusalem, Bethlehem and
the Dead Sea—the area where David tended the flock of
his father Jesse—was a place full of all these dangers.

This is why David refers to it in Psalm 23 as the "valley
of the shadow of death." He understood from personal
experience that whenever he and his sheep were moving
through a valley, they were walking in the shadow of all
kinds of impending peril. In the valleys, possible death
hung over him and his flock like a "shadow."

It occurred to me, as I was studying this verse, that as
God's sheep, we walk through similar valleys every day.
Remember, the "valley of the shadow of death" doesn't
mean just those valleys where we are actually dying. It
refers to those valleys where we are exposed and

vulnerable to the *possibility* of death. And indeed, isn't this true of us every day? Every day, don't we walk through a world where death is possible at any turn?

But on a more specific level, I also think that the "valley of the shadow of death" is talking about those dark and difficult crisis experiences of life that we face from time to time. It refers to places in life where things appear unknown and threatening and precarious and dangerous, like a new valley always looked to sheep. Even as God's sheep, we're going to have these deep valleys in our lives. Jesus told us this in John 16:33: "In the world you have tribulation." David said the same thing: "Many are the afflictions of the righteous" (Psalm 34:19).

My wife and I have been going through just such a valley since 1992 when our Jill was born. As her condition worsened, the medical expenses decimated our personal finances. On several occasions, Jill's death seemed imminent. We were in the valley where *real* death lived. All the while, we tried hard to make sure we were giving enough time and emotional energy to our three healthy boys (ages 15, 11 and 7 when Jill was born), but there simply wasn't enough of us to go around. We found ourselves in the deepest, darkest valley of our lives—so deep that we often referred to it as "the black hole."

Most of us don't like valleys like this. We'd like to go from mountaintop to mountaintop by helicopter! But life doesn't work that way. The only way to get from one mountaintop to another is by walking through a valley. That's not only normal human geography; it's also God's spiritual geography. It's simply the way God runs things.

However, I have learned something very important about valleys. I have learned that valleys can also be precious places for us as God's sheep. Oftentimes, the grass is the greenest in the valley. Oftentimes, the presence of the shepherd is sweetest in the valley. Oftentimes, we learn more about the character and personhood of our shepherd in the valley than we do on the hillside. You see, valleys are inevitable for God's sheep, but they are not necessarily bad things. There is no reason to fear the valleys if we understand the remedy God is offering us for the fears and stresses we find there.

This leads us to the second part of this verse: "Yea, though I walk through the valley of the shadow of death [and you will, and so will I], I will fear no evil." How can a person pass through perilous places like this and have no fear? David tells us the answer. It is, simply, "for You are with me."

Remember what we said earlier. True security for sheep is not found in the absence of danger but in the presence of the shepherd. And for God's sheep, the same is certainly true. God tells us that the solution to our fear when we're in the deep valleys is the assurance of his presence with us.

We have seen how God restores our souls and how he guides us. The issue here in verse 4 is security—protection. God protects his sheep.

Sheep are very timid animals. They are easily frightened and totally without the means to defend themselves. The only reason that the sheep in Israel would walk through the valleys slowly and leisurely is because they could see that their shepherd was with them at every moment. He knew the way. He would get them through safely. It was the presence of the shepherd that calmed all their fears.

This is the same security that God offers us as his sheep. He assures us that he will be with us at every moment. Jesus promised us this in Hebrews 13:5: "I WILL NEVER DESERT

YOU, NOR WILL I EVER FORSAKE YOU." God knows the way and
promises that he will lead us through safely. This is the only
security that God offers his sheep. But this is the only
security we need.

Throughout the ages, when people facing the spiritual
valley before them were scared and gripped with fear, God
always said the same thing to them. He always offered
them the identical solution to their fear. He said to them all,
"Fear not." And the reason was, "For I am with you."

When Abraham was feeling insecure and alone in the
land of Canaan, God appeared to him and said, "Do not
fear, for I am with you" (Genesis 26:24). When God called
Jacob to return to Canaan and face his brother Esau whom
he had cheated, Jacob was terrified that Esau was going to
kill him on sight. In response, God said to Jacob, "I will be
with you" (Genesis 31:3). In Numbers 14, Caleb was trying
to persuade the Israelites to obey God and invade the
Promised Land. The people were frozen with fear over the
reports of how large and powerful the inhabitants of the
land were. In seeking to assuage their fear, Caleb said to
them, "Do not fear the people of the land . . . the LORD is
with us" (Numbers 14:9).

And how about the people who, when God asked
them to do something for him, replied by saying, "I can't.
It's too much. I'm too frightened." What did God say to
every one of these folks?

At the burning bush, when Moses began to give God
all the reasons why he couldn't possibly go face
Pharaoh, God said to him, "Certainly I will be with you"
(Exodus 3:12). When Gideon was afraid to attack the
Midianites, God said to him, "Surely I will be with you"
(Judges 6:16). When King Jehoshaphat looked out from
the ramparts of Jerusalem and saw the armies of three
nations surrounding the city, he felt powerless and did

not know what to do. But when he cried out to God, God spoke to him through a prophet, who said to him and all of Judah, "Do not fear or be dismayed . . . for the LORD is with you" (2 Chronicles 20:17).

Friends, this is what God has said to everybody who was afraid of the valley. This is what he has said to everyone who felt impotent to do what God asked him or her to do. He didn't give these people a pop psychology lecture or offer them speeches full of psychobabble. He didn't throw feel-good flattery at them or try to infuse courage into them with the power of positive thinking. What's more, he didn't try to convince them that the dangers they were afraid of weren't real. He simply said to them, "No matter what happens, I will be with you— and I'm bigger than any danger you may be facing."

That's all they needed to know. And, what's really cool is that in every case God backed up his promise with action. Hand in hand, God led every one of these people through the valley safely and victoriously, just as he said he would.

As God's sheep in the modern world, it doesn't matter what we're facing or how rough it is or how scared we are. God gives every one of us the very same assurance and hope that he gave Abraham, Moses, Joshua and Jacob—namely, "I will be with you." That's all you and I need to know. That's all we need to hear. Knowing that God is with us, every moment of every day in every situation of life, should bring joy and confidence to every one of God's sheep.

When Brenda and I were in the worst moments of the "black hole" with little Jill, it was this wonderful truth that kept us going. I'll never forget one night, standing in the emergency room at 3 A.M. with my wife. Jill had suffered several severe grand mals and we had frantically transported her to the hospital. Just as we arrived, she stopped breathing and the staff rushed her into a room and began to use a bag valve mask to try to get her breathing again. As Brenda and I stood outside in the hallway by ourselves, not sure whether our daughter was going to survive the night, feeling despondent and very alone, I put my arm around my wife and remembered the words of God: "Fear not, for I am with you." Suddenly, I had this overwhelming sense that there were *three* of us standing there in that sterile hallway—me with my arm around Brenda, and Jesus with his arm around both of us.

I can't really explain in words how this spiritual realization changed my feelings from despair to hope. All I can tell you is that it did.

It was the presence of the Good Shepherd that changed that night from bleakness into hope. Just like Jesus said, "Peace, be still" to the waves on the Sea of Galilee and the waves complied, so his presence at 3 A.M. said, "Peace, be still" to my beleaguered soul and my soul complied. It was like being back in my dark bedroom and hearing my dad say, "Son, I'm right here with you. So relax. There's nothing to be afraid of. I'll handle everything."

Now to make this kind of confident assertion— "There's nothing to be afraid of. I'll handle everything"— demands a huge amount of power to back it up. And that leads us to the third and final part of this verse: "Your rod and Your staff, they comfort me."

Now what in the world does this mean? Well, it means that God has all the equipment necessary to do the job of protecting us.

You see, someone might be tempted to look at God and say, "Gee, that's sure nice that you tell me you're with me in everything. But how do I know that your being with me makes all that much difference? I mean, somebody might come along and overcome us *both*. So what good is that?"

It's like the deal with my dad as a child. I derived great comfort from his assurance that he was there for me. I believed my dad could handle anything. But now I realize that the kind of green, hairy monsters that I was afraid of could have eaten both me and my dad—no problem! You see, when it came to providing real security and freedom from fear, my dad's presence was only as good as his power.

This is the great thing about being one of God's sheep: *our* shepherd can handle anything. This is what David means when he says, "Your rod and Your staff, they comfort me."

What are these two items? The rod was a clublike weapon that would often have nails in one end of it. Shepherds, from the time they were little, would practice using this club. They became so adept at using it that they could throw it with amazing accuracy. The shepherd did not use the rod on his sheep—he used it on their enemies!

I think of David's words to King Saul as David prepared to go out and face Goliath: "When a lion or a bear came and took a lamb from the flock, I went out after him . . . and when he rose up against me, I seized him by his beard and struck him and killed him" (1 Samuel 17:34–35). I used to think that David merely hit the predator with his hand. But now I realize that this isn't what David did at all. He hit the beast with his club—the rod. The sheep knew that as long as the shepherd had his rod in his hand, they could relax, because he had all the firepower needed to protect them.

We as God's sheep can take similar comfort in the fact that God has a rod too. In the Bible, God refers to it as a

"rod of iron." It's a rod that consists of his omnipotence.
It's a rod that comes from his irresistible will and power
that no creature in the universe can oppose.

King Nebuchadnezzar of Babylon came to understand
how big God's rod is after God turned him into a babbling,
senseless creature for months. When he recovered his
senses, he declared of God: "for His dominion is an
everlasting dominion. . . . All the inhabitants of the earth
are accounted as nothing . . . He does according to His will
in the host of heaven and among the inhabitants of earth;
and no one can ward off His hand or say to Him, 'What
have You done?'" (Daniel 4:34–35). Nebuchadnezzar's
point is quite simple: God wields a big "rod."

The Bible leaves no doubt about this: anything God
wants to happen will happen. There's no trouble we'll
ever find ourselves in, no enemy who will ever come
against us, no valley we'll ever have to cross—that the
rod of God can't deal with. It's an almighty rod.

But, you know, every trouble that sheep get into
doesn't come from without. Sheep have an incredible
ability to get in trouble from within! They don't need a
lion or a bear. They don't need snakes or robbers or
flash floods. Sheep can get entangled in brambles or
stuck in bushes. They can wander off and get disoriented
or fall off craggy cliffs. They can easily get lost and be
unable to find their way back home. Sheep can do a lot
of things all by themselves to get in trouble.

So, beside the rod, the shepherd has another piece of
equipment. He's got the staff.

We all know what a shepherd's staff looks like. It's a
long pole with a little curved crook at the top. It was this
crook that the shepherd used to help the sheep when
they got themselves into trouble. If sheep got in the
middle of the brambles, the shepherd would reach down

and grab them gently around the neck and pull them out. If sheep got close to a cliff or precipice, the shepherd would reach out with his staff and pull them back to safety. If sheep started to wander off where they shouldn't, the shepherd would reach out with his staff and coax them back into the flock.

Now, not only does the rod provide comfort, but the staff does also. And that comfort extends to us. It means that God promises to keep us from wandering off and getting ourselves into trouble of our own making.

So what is the staff of God? We understand the rod very well. It's God's power and omnipotence. But what is the staff of God? Some have suggested that the staff is his Word, the Bible, because by paying heed to its teachings, we stay close to the flock and the shepherd. This is why David said in Psalm 119:105 that God's Word is "a lamp to my feet and a light to my path." By reading and obeying the Bible, God keeps us from wandering into the spiritual brambles and off the spiritual precipices of life. And certainly this is part of the answer.

But I believe another big part of God's staff are the guardian angels that God assigns to every one of his sheep. As a follower of Christ, did you realize that the Bible says you have at least one angel assigned to guard and protect you? Maybe some of us have more than one. In fact, I have one son who, growing up, needed an entire platoon of angels!

Hebrews 1:14 tells us that angels are "ministering spirits, sent out to render service for the sake of those who will inherit salvation." In Matthew 18:10, Jesus, talking about children, God's "little ones," says, "their angels in heaven continually see the face of My Father who is in heaven." This explains why children actually make it to adulthood. Children do the most reckless and mindless things—things that expose them to constant dangers and even death. The reason children actually survive and grow up is because their guardian angels help them.

Psalm 91:11–12 tells us, "For He will give His angels charge concerning you, to guard you in all your ways. They will bear you up in their hands, that you do not strike your foot against a stone." Now I know we don't think much about it, but when we drive down the highway, there is always an angel "riding shotgun" with us. Everywhere we go and everything we do, we have our guardian angel(s) there with us. Their mission is to watch over us and protect us even from ourselves.

Psalm 34:7 says, "The angel of the LORD encamps around those who fear Him, and rescues them." In Genesis 24:7 Abraham says to his servant: "He will send His angel before you." In Exodus 14:19 we find that there was an angel who went before the Israelites and led them. When they arrived at the Red Sea, the Bible says that the angel moved behind them and protected them from the Egyptians. In 1 Kings 19:5–7, when Elijah was emotionally down and depressed and about to wander away and get himself in trouble spiritually, the Bible says that God sent an angel to minister to him and kept Elijah from self-destructing.

I believe that this ministry of guardian angels forms a major portion of the staff of God. They help keep us in line, they remind us of God's truth and encourage us to observe it, they hem us in and move us along and protect us even from ourselves. Some of us work our angels overtime. Others of us are easier on our angels. But either way, they are there to walk along with us and protect us.

In summary, where does all this leave us?

Well, the Bible says we're going to walk through some valleys in life as God's sheep. But we don't need to be afraid, because God has promised to always be with us. God's got a big "rod," his omnipotence and power, to protect us. He's got a staff, his Word and guardian angels, to keep us from wandering into the ditches of life on our own.

What should our response be to all this?

David summed up his response in three simple words: "I will trust." Everywhere we read about David in the Bible, we find him always saying the same thing about God: "I will trust him." In Psalm 56:3, David said, "When I am afraid, I will put my trust in You." In Psalm 27:1, he said, "The LORD is the defense of my life; whom shall I dread?" The prophet Isaiah responded in the same way: "Behold, God is my salvation, I will trust and not be afraid" (Isaiah 12:2).

To fear no evil while walking through the valley of the shadow of death is the inheritance of every follower of Jesus Christ. And the secret to making this inheritance ours is "I will trust."

It's of little use to know Psalm 23:4 if we're not willing to appropriate it by trusting the God who made the promise. This is where so many of us run into problems. If God promised he'd protect us, he will. If God said he'd be with us, he will. Trust him. And God will see you through just like a shepherd sees his sheep through.

Some of us reading this are in the middle of some tough valleys right now. We feel like we're at the bottom of the "black hole," like Brenda and I did for years. Please allow me to encourage you with this fact. The valley is only a passageway. Flocks in ancient Israel didn't camp or permanently reside in the valleys. The valley was merely a pathway to higher ground. The same is true in our walk with God. God only uses the valleys in our lives as a way to get us to higher ground spiritually.

This means that every valley God leads us into, no

matter how deep and bleak it may look, is only
temporary. It's just a passageway, and passageways, by
definition, aren't permanent.

Brenda and I really wondered if we would ever see
the end of the valley we were in with our daughter, Jill.
We honestly questioned if we'd ever laugh again, if we'd
ever smile again, if we'd ever be happy again. But when
Jill was eight years old, a doctor finally determined that
she has a genetic disease and, even though it cannot be
fixed, he has been able to control the seizures with
certain treatments. Jill has begun to learn a few new
skills and has stabilized in a way that we never dreamed
possible a few years ago. Even though life can still be
challenging and difficult as we care for Jill, by God's
grace and mercy we are through the valley and out of
the "black hole." And as we look back, we can see the
wonderful way in which God led us through the valley
of the shadow of death.

Were there times we were so scared that we didn't
know what to do? Absolutely. Were there times we were
paralyzed with fear and insecurity? Sure. But we decided
that we were going to trust God to keep his promises.
And he did.

If you'll trust God in your valleys, then one day when
you step on the shores of heaven (if not before), you're
going to look back and say, "Hey, I made it and God
was utterly faithful all the way, just like he said he'd be."

May God encourage you in the valleys of life. God
said he'd be with you. He promised he'd protect you.
Trust him and he'll do what he said.

*Lord Jesus, I am a frightened little sheep, afraid of my
own shadow sometimes. I may act tough on the outside, but
on the inside I am consumed with fears and insecurities.*

This is why I am so thankful for your promise of Psalm 23:4. In your words "You are with me," I find enormous comfort and confidence. Those words reassure me at a spiritual level that is unreachable by any human philosophy or insipid schemes of man. It is the constant presence of the shepherd that bolsters the sheep and it is your everlasting presence that bolsters me.

As I walk through the valley of the shadow of death, please help me to believe you and trust you with all my heart. Please teach me that "Jesus is all I need." Thank you for the deep valleys, where you are able to teach people this great truth as in no other place. Please cause me to remember that the valleys are merely pathways to higher ground. Help me not to despise them but to embrace them as part of your inscrutable and perfect plan for me as your sheep.

Remind me, Lord, that you have been utterly faithful to every sheep you ever owned—and you will be utterly faithful to me. In Jesus' name, Amen!

PART SIX

YOU PREPARE A TABLE BEFORE ME

**. . . in the presence of my enemies.
You anoint my head with oil.
My cup runs over.**

It is widely believed that, in this verse, David leaves the imagery of sheep and shepherds and turns to the imagery of a great banquet.

At this banquet, God sets a beautiful dinner table in front of us as his guests. As our enemies look on with envy, God the host anoints our heads with fragrant oil as an act of kindness and affection. He then fills our drink glasses to overflowing abundance as an act of generosity and benevolence. The point of the verse, then, would be to communicate to everyone watching how favored we are in the sight of God when we are followers of his.

For many years, this is exactly how I looked at this verse: as a lovely banquet. But that's not how I see it anymore. I am certain that David is still talking about sheep and shepherds in this verse, not a great banquet.

You might ask, "Okay then, Lon, so then what do tables and oil and cups have to do with sheep?" Well, let's look carefully at what David says and I believe we'll get our answer.

Now remember, in verse 4 we said it was spring and summertime. The sheep have left their winter quarters and headed up toward the high ground in the mountains for their summer grazing. Normally barren in the winter, these hilltops come to life with all kinds of rich vegetation in the spring. So the shepherd is taking his sheep up onto those high places to graze in lush, green pastures.

These pastures are what David refers to in verse 5 as a "table." The word can be better translated here as "tableland." Tablelands are those much sought-after grazing places high in the mountains. Even in America today, especially in the West, we hear talk about tablelands and mesas. A "mesa" is simply a Spanish word that means "table" or "tableland." These are the rich grazing spots where the shepherd took his sheep for their spring and summer habitat.

So then, David's phrase "You prepare a table before me in the presence of my enemies" has nothing to do with a human banquet. It has to do with the rich pastures that the shepherd prepares for his flock to feed in.

Now you might say, "But, Lon, I thought you said that these were just mountain fields that spontaneously sprung to life on their own every spring. I thought you said that the shepherd simply leads his sheep up to these places and then sits in the shade drinking his Dr. Pepper while they graze. What kind of *preparation* is David talking about?"

Well, this idyllic scene of the shepherd just showing up at perfectly prepared tableland is not accurate. Actually, long before his sheep ever arrive at these tablelands, the shepherd has been involved in getting them ready for his sheep.

Early in the spring he goes up to these mesas and

searches out the best sections for his sheep. He decides ahead of time exactly where the best places are to set up camp. The shepherd makes several trips to bring up the raw materials he'll need to build those summer camps. He also has to distribute salt and minerals over the pasture so that, in the middle of the hot summer, his sheep will have the nutrients they need to stay healthy. He cleans out the water holes of all the leaves, twigs and debris that have collected in them over the winter. He gets rid of the algae so that his sheep have clean, clear water to drink. He checks for poisonous plants that may have grown up and eradicates them where he can. Where this is not possible, he fences off those sections of the pastureland so that his sheep will not eat these poisonous plants and become ill.

In short, when David says "You prepare a table before me," he is speaking of the preparation work that the shepherd does to these mountain pastures before his sheep ever arrive there.

In his book *A Shepherd Looks at Psalm 23*, Phillip Keller tells about doing this very thing for his sheep:

> The first sheep ranch I owned had a rather prolific native stand of both blue and white cammas. The blue cammas were a delightful sight in the spring when they bloomed along the beaches. The white cammas, though a much less conspicuous flower, were also quite attractive, but a deadly menace to sheep. If lambs, in particular, ate or even just nibbled a few of the lily-like leaves . . . it would spell certain death. The lambs would become paralyzed, stiffen up like blocks of wood and simply succumb to the toxic poisons from the plants. My youngsters and I spent days and days going over the ground plucking out these poisonous

plants. It was a recurring task that was done every
spring before the sheep went on these pastures.
Though tedious and tiring with all of the bending . . .
if my sheep were to survive it simply had to be done.[9]

David also mentions in this verse that the shepherd
prepared the tablelands for his sheep in the presence of
their enemies. He is referring to the work that the shepherd
did to deal with predators who were anxious to prey on his
sheep up on the mesas. He would run off snakes, killing
them if possible, destroying their nests and their young. He
would scout out the places where cougars or lions or
coyotes could lie in wait for his sheep. He would carefully
reconnoiter the whole area for ambush spots where thieves
could hide in preparation for stealing all or part of the flock.

As a result of his thorough preparation, when the
sheep were grazing, the shepherd knew exactly where
the danger points were. Even in the presence of the
sheep's enemies, David says, the shepherd is way ahead
of things. He has gone ahead of the sheep and already
taken care of all the potential pitfalls for them. All this
preparation had to be completed before the shepherd
ever took a single sheep up into the highlands to graze.
David, no doubt, had done this very thing countless
times for his father's sheep.

To put it another way, the shepherd had to outthink the
dangers and be steps ahead of the sheep. The shepherd
couldn't just lead his sheep up to the tablelands and then
play it by ear. He had to be way ahead of the curve if he
wanted to ensure his sheep's safety and security. When the
sheep finally arrived at the mesa, they had the confidence
that their shepherd had already been there, inspected it,
defused its dangers and made it a safe place.

This is precisely what David is saying God does for

his sheep. God, just like a good shepherd, goes ahead of his sheep and prepares the tablelands where he is planning to lead us, so that when we arrive there, it is a safe and secure place.

For those of us who are God's sheep, the Bible declares that God is so far ahead of us that it isn't even funny. When we enter into a tough situation in life and we say, "My goodness, look at this"—we need to remember that God has been there long before we ever arrived. He's been there preparing that experience for us, making sure that it will be safe for us, ensuring that it will contribute positively to our spiritual growth and development and establishing spiritual fences so that no enemy can injure us there.

God declares in Psalm 139:16 that he knows everything that is going to happen in our lives before we were ever born. God says that he has already inspected every detail of our life and prepared every situation we will ever find ourselves in, just like the shepherd did for his sheep up on the tablelands.

God has anticipated every danger we will ever face and has fashioned a solution before we ever get there. God has seen every crisis and is aware of every need we will ever have—and he has already been through the mesas of our life making provision for them all. This is what David is trying to tell us. He's trying to say, "Part of being one of God's sheep means that wherever I end up on the path of life, I can be absolutely sure that my Good Shepherd has already been there ahead of me and made it a safe place for me to be."

When I think of this great truth, I think of Peter. Not long before his arrest and crucifixion, Jesus said to Peter, "Simon, Simon, behold, Satan has demanded permission to sift you like wheat; but I have prayed for you, that your faith may not fail" (Luke 22:31–32).

Notice that the event Jesus is speaking about hasn't even happened yet. Jesus is referring to the events surrounding his arrest and trial in Jerusalem, during which Peter would deny him three times. Now Peter has no idea that this is even coming. But—and here's the critical point—Jesus knew all about it way in advance. Jesus had already been to that place in Peter's life. Jesus had already seen what was ahead for Peter. Jesus had prayed for Peter and Peter's faith. Jesus had already planned how he was going to restore Peter's confidence and recommission Peter's service for God after Peter acted unfaithfully. Just like David says here in Psalm 23, Jesus had already made provision for his sheep's survival. This is why Jesus went on to tell Peter, "when once you have turned again, strengthen your brothers" (Luke 22:32). Jesus could say this to Peter because he already knew that Peter *would* turn back to God.

Now I'm sure that upon hearing these words from Jesus, Peter must have wondered what in the world was going on—what did Jesus know was coming. But Jesus simply wanted Peter to know, and he wants you and me to know, that he is way ahead of us. It's as though Jesus were saying to Peter, "Hey, pal, I'm so far ahead of you that it's not even funny. You have no idea what's going to happen yet, but I do. I know about it all. And I've already made provision for you, Peter. I've already taken steps to make sure that you are protected even in this unfortunate situation. I've made provision so that you have a way through it that preserves your faith, your dignity and your personhood. I've already made sure that your Enemy won't be able to use this situation to destroy you. You may not like what's about to happen to you, Peter, but you're going to be safe in it and you're going to develop into a deeper man of God through it. I've already taken care of everything to these ends. So relax and don't be afraid."

In these words, Jesus is trying to teach Peter that he can trust God, because anywhere Peter goes in life, God's already been there. He's trying to reassure Peter that, even though the road might sometimes get bumpy, God has acted in advance and put just the right kind of shock absorbers on Peter's chariot.

And the big "So what?" for us here is that this is the exact same assurance that God wants us to have as we move through life. God wants us to know that he has already prepared the tablelands before us in the presence of our enemies. He has already been everywhere we should go. He has already made sure that it's safe for us to be there. He's already planned out how he's going to get us through these situations, what he's going to teach us in these situations and how he's going to protect us from all danger in these situations.

God is way ahead of you and me, just like he was for Peter, just like every good shepherd is for his sheep.

I know this is true because I have seen it firsthand in my life in so many times. Back in 1980, I had agreed to come to McLean Bible Church to serve as senior pastor. Brenda and I were living in Crofton, Maryland, at the time (a suburb of Washington, D.C., about 45 minutes driving time from the church building), and we had not yet sold our home there. But we decided to take a chance and buy a home in northern Virginia anyway. We were certain our Maryland home would sell and so we went for it.

Well, our Maryland home *didn't* sell and we were in big trouble. Our closing on the new house was fast approaching and the only way we could go to settlement was to have the funds that we expected to take away from selling the Maryland house. We were praying and praying and asking God to intervene. We realized that if our home didn't sell, or something else didn't happen, we were going to default on our Virginia purchase. Great beginning, right? New pastor defaults on real estate contract!

About a week before D-Day (that is, "default day"), we got a call from my wife's folks. They knew about the situation but there wasn't much they could do financially to help. However, my wife's grandmother, who had been involved in a very lucrative business with Brenda's grandfather, had called up Brenda's parents the night before with a strange request.

She had said to them, "You know, I was praying just the other night on my knees. I had some money coming up for renewal in a CD and it was a lot of money. I was praying about what to do with it and how to reinvest it. And as I was on my knees, I really sensed from the Lord that I needed to call you first. I sensed that I needed to ask you if any of the grandchildren need any financial help right now."

Brenda's mom said, "Well, now that you mention it (she had never said a word to Brenda's grandmother before this), Brenda and Lon are in a little bit of a pinch." Brenda's mom then went on to explain the whole situation and how we needed a big chunk of money to make the down payment on the new home. Brenda's dear grandmother said, "It's no problem. My CD is coming to maturity on Friday (D-day was Monday!). I'll just take some of the cash out and give it to Lon and Brenda to use. They can pay me a low rate of interest, and when they finally sell their Maryland home, they can pay me back."

God rescued us big-time! And I'll be honest with you, I was really sweating it!

But when all this happened with Brenda's

grandmother, I learned a critical lesson as a follower of God. I learned that God was already way ahead of me on this. He had already been to this crisis, seen it and worked out a way through it. He had orchestrated every detail, even down to having the grandmother's CD come to maturity right on the weekend before I needed it. This encouraged my faith so much, because I thought, *Lord, if you had all this worked out like this before I even got here, then there is nothing in life that I have to fear. I don't need to worry about anything, because you've already prepared every mesa for me before I'm even going to arrive at it. I just need to take it as it comes and trust you, God.*

May I say to you, I don't know what problem or crisis or situation you may be facing right now. But I can promise you that God is way ahead of you. He's already visited it. He's already prepared the water holes and spread out the minerals there. He's already uprooted the poisonous plants. He's already run the snakes off and cleared out the predators. He's already made sure that, in spite of the threats of danger that are all around, you're going to be safe.

He's way ahead of you! He's already prepared this tableland for you before you ever arrived to accomplish your spiritual growth and welfare. You may not like or want the situation that you find yourself in. The journey may not be an easy one. But be assured that it is a "prepared journey." And if you'll just trust your Good Shepherd, when it's all over, he will have proved this to you in spades.

Okay, now let's take a look at the second part of this verse: "You anoint my head with oil."

Again, I believe that the secret to understanding this phrase properly is to understand sheep and shepherds.

Even though the sheep are grazing contentedly up on the tablelands, even though they are safely feeding in rich pastures, even though the shepherd is protecting them from predators and poisons, the sheep still had to face a host of smaller enemies.

None of these enemies were deadly, but they could be unbelievably annoying. These enemies were the parasites and pests and flies and mosquitoes and gnats and lice that love to attack sheep.

One of the worst nuisances to sheep up in the mesas were "nose flies." These were flies that would try to lay their eggs in the soft, moist membranes of the sheep's noses. When their eggs would hatch, the little larvae would creep up into the sheep's nasal passages and burrow in. This wouldn't kill the sheep, but it was extremely painful. Sheep will often be seen beating their heads against posts and rocks trying to get some relief from these larvae.

Another big problem was a highly contagious skin disease, similar to the mange, which the shepherds called "scab." This disease caused the sheep's hair to fall out and the skin to become irritated. Sheep would often get it on their heads because they have a tendency to nuzzle one another with their heads, making this the point of contact where the disease can be passed from one animal to another.

All of these smaller pests could turn a summer into a very tortuous time for the sheep. The antidote for all these little pests was oil, not just any oil but a very special mixture. The shepherds of ancient Israel used an oil that was mixed with spices and sulfur. You say, "Sulfur? Man, those sheep must have really stunk!" Well, I suspect that's true; as we all know, sulfur smells like rotten eggs. But I'd much rather smell like rotten eggs than have nose flies, scabs, lice and gnats all over me! And I'm sure sheep feel the same way.

Shepherds would smear this ointment all over their sheep. They gave special attention to the sheep's head, of course, since this is where so many of these pests focused their attack. The shepherd would rub this special oil in by hand. He did this repeatedly over the days and weeks of the summer. By doing this, it would keep all these nasty little pests away from his sheep. This was all part of the shepherd's loving care and provision for his sheep.

So when God says in Psalm 23 that he anoints our heads with oil, what is he really saying?

What he is saying is that not only does he go ahead of us and take care of the big things in life for us (like snakes and poison plants and lions), but he also takes care of the little things, like the flies and gnats and scab. God is not only concerned about the things in life that can kill and destroy us. He also cares about the things that are simply nuisances and annoyances—things that weigh down our hearts and sap our joy and burden our souls. And God has provided for them too.

I mean, think about the things you pray for. I'll bet that most of them are not life-threatening situations. I'll bet that the vast majority of them involve problems and situations that are simply burdensome, frustrating and painfully heavy on your heart.

Sometime these things may relate to your children or your job or your health or your relationships with others. Maybe they deal with school or sports or your car or your house. And you go to God with these and pray, "Lord, please deal with these burdens in my life." What we're really asking God to do in these prayers is to "anoint our heads with oil." We're asking him to deal with the annoyances and everyday burdens of life.

The great news of the Bible is that God is never too busy or too distracted to help us in these ways. Although these issues are minor in comparison to global hunger and nuclear proliferation, if they are important to us, then they are important to our heavenly shepherd.

It's just like being a parent. Because of how deeply we love our children, whatever is important to them immediately becomes important to us. Because of our love for them, we proactively engage in helping our children with these issues, regardless of how trivial they might appear to a bystander. In Psalm 23, David says that this is exactly how God reacts to us.

This is why David exclaimed, "Blessed be the Lord, who daily bears our burden" (Psalm 68:19). This is why Jesus invited us to "come to me, all who are weary and heavy-laden" (Matthew 11:28). They don't have to be big cares or life-threatening cares. They can be just little cares, but annoying cares just the same. "And," Jesus continues, "I will give you rest." "I'll give you a respite from those cares."

This is why Paul said in Philippians 4:6–7, "Be anxious for nothing, but in everything by prayer and supplication with thanksgiving let your requests [big and small alike] be made known to God. And the peace of God, which surpasses all comprehension, will guard your hearts and your minds in Christ Jesus." It's why David said, "Cast your burden upon the Lord and He will sustain you" (Psalm 55:2).

To summarize: With the big problems in life, God loves to prepare the tablelands before us in the very presence of dangers and enemies, so that we can walk through those dangers safely. With the little problems of life, God loves to rub his special oil on his sheep and to run off those annoyances. And the wonderful truth is that none of these issues, whether big or small, ever catch God by surprise. He's already aware of each need we will ever face and he has already made perfect provision for every situation into which his sheep arrive.

Finally, David decides to sum up everything he's trying to communicate here with the simple assertion: "My cup runs over."

Just as David did in verse 3, where he said, "He [God] restores my soul," David departs from his sheep-shepherd imagery for a moment here at the end of verse 5 to make sure that we get the point. He simply and straightforwardly declares, "My cup is so full with God's tender, anticipatory care that it's positively overflowing."

With his words here in verse 5, David challenges each of us to reflect on God's incredible plan for our lives. He challenges us to appreciate how perfectly and precisely God has gone ahead of us and planned out every detail with a synchronization that is uncanny.

And that's just part of it. Not only has God planned things out in advance for our general safety and comfort in life, but he has gone far beyond that. In God's kindness and grace, his plan for his sheep includes luxuries and privileges that go far beyond our basic necessities. He's planned things out with such generosity and beneficence that "our cups run over."

You know, in John 10:10, Jesus declares that he has come "that they may have life, and have it abundantly." Did you ever notice that this promise is found embedded in the passage where Jesus declares himself to be our Good Shepherd? In fact, right after this promise, Jesus says in verse 11, "I am the good shepherd."

I don't believe that the close connection of these two statements is coincidental. Not at all. Abundant life is the kind of life that every shepherd wants for his sheep. It's the ultimate mark of success for a shepherd: the more abundant life his sheep enjoy, the more he has succeeded in his role as their shepherd. Nothing gives a human shepherd more satisfaction than to see his sheep living abundant lives.

In the same way, the Bible tells us that nothing gives God more joy than to see us, as his followers, flourishing. This explains why God says to us in Psalm 81:10, "Open your mouth wide and I will fill it."

This is not a life verse for dentists! It's a life verse for God's sheep! God is telling us as his sheep that if we'll open our mouths wide and simply show childlike trust in him, he will fill our mouths to overflowing, not just with material blessings but with spiritual blessings too. In this regard, I love the last stanza of that fabulous hymn "Great Is Thy Faithfulness":

> Pardon for sin and a peace that endureth,
> Thine own dear presence to cheer and to guide;
> Strength for today and bright hope for tomorrow,
> Blessings all mine with ten thousand beside![10]

This is the way God gives—generously, abundantly, overflowing.

Recently, I was sitting on the beach with my oldest son, James, and we were talking as we watched the sun set in glorious fashion. I said to him, "You know, James, there's really nothing I ever dreamed about, or desired even as a luxury, that the Lord hasn't given me. I have a beautiful, godly, faithful wife. I have three wonderful boys and one daughter-in-law who all love the Lord and are living honorable, productive lives. Little Jill is stabilized and doing better than she's ever done. I'm about to become a grandfather, thanks to you and your wife. I've got a lovely home and two nice cars. I serve an incredible church family who love me in spite of myself.

I've got good health and strength to live every day. God
is using my life to make a difference for Jesus Christ in
this world. I've got the sure promise of heaven when I
leave earth. I've been to Israel over twenty times; I've
walked many times where Paul walked in Greece and
Turkey, and where Moses walked in Egypt. I mean,
honestly, if you were to ask me, son, what I really want
that I don't have—I couldn't think of much."

After a pause I went on, "And you know what is the
most amazing part of it all? It's that I began my walk with
God over 30 years ago with $5 in my pocket, literally, and
in the 30-plus years since, I've never done anything but
ministry. I've never made big money as a CEO or had
stock options or platinum parachutes. And yet, look what
the Lord has given me and your mom."

And it's true, my friends. I stand in utter amazement of
how I got all the wonderful spiritual blessings and
material stuff I have today. I never set out with the goal
of getting all this. I simply set out with the goal of being a
faithful sheep of Jesus Christ. There have been some
rough times, for sure. But I want to tell everyone reading
this book that God doesn't owe me a thing!

God has gone ahead of me and done the kind of
advance planning of my life, such that, truly, "my cup
runs over." If God were to take me home right now, I
could leave, declaring that "my cup runs over." There's
not been a thing I've needed over the years as his sheep
that God hasn't provided for me. Moreover, there have
hardly been any luxuries that I ever dreamed about that
God hasn't graciously sent my way as well in his perfect
timing. It's as the hymn writer said:

> Praise ye the Lord, who o'er all things so
> wondrously reigneth,

Shelters thee under His wings, yea so gently
sustaineth!
Hast thou not seen how thy desires e'er have been
Granted in what He ordaineth?[11]

Now, if you've been one of God's sheep for any
length of time, I'll bet you can say the same thing. Just
like me, God's advance planning of your life has resulted
in your having, not only everything you've needed, but a
bunch of stuff you didn't really need that God gave you
anyway. This is all because of the fact that God agreed to
take us on as his sheep. And as the ultimate Good
Shepherd, one of God's highest aims is our well-being
and prosperity as his sheep, materially and spiritually.

And so, please let me challenge you. We have to trust
God. We have to trust his advance planning for our lives,
as he said in Jeremiah 29:11, "'For I know the plans that I
have for you,' declares the LORD, 'plans for welfare and
not for calamity to give you a future and a hope.'"

Sometimes things don't go the way we want them to.
Sometimes the pathway upon which God leads us is
painful and difficult. Sometimes God's plan for us seems
nonsensical and arbitrary. That's okay. Just remember that
the Good Shepherd is way ahead of us, just like he was
for Peter. And if we'll trust him and simply follow his
leading, the end result will always be a cup that runs over.

*Lord, I want to give you my personal thanks because
you have provided for me in ways that 30-plus years ago I
could never have imagined. You've given me things that,
on the human level, I really didn't need. They might have
been things I wanted, but, Lord, we both know I could
have made it fine without them. And yet, in your mercy,
you chose to give them to me anyway. You have given to*

me so richly that, indeed, I can say, "my cup runs over."

Lord, I don't believe you've given these things to me for any other reason than the simple fact that I'm your sheep and you're my shepherd. As I've been willing to just let go of control and trust you with my life, you've given to me the only way you know how—and that's abundantly.

Father, I pray for every person reading this book, that you would impress this same gratitude upon each one. And even though many of us may not understand the situations that we're facing right now, teach us to embrace them and thank you for them by faith, because we are confident that you have already been here.

You have already inspected and prepared these places for us. You have already made a safe way through each place, and you already have planned how each of these experiences is going to contribute to our cup running over in the future. And even if we can't see how right now, assure us that one day we are guaranteed to see it, because you have promised it is so and you cannot lie.

Father, help us to stop worrying about the future, because you have already been to the future for each of us. Help us to simply enjoy the riches that you have provided for us here in the present.

Father, great is your faithfulness. There is nothing we as your sheep will ever need that you won't provide. Nor will those needs ever surprise you, because you have already completed the advance planning of our lives.

You are the Good Shepherd, Lord, and we are honored to be your sheep. In Jesus' name, we pray. Amen.

PART SEVEN

SURELY GOODNESS AND MERCY SHALL FOLLOW ME

**. . . all the days of my life;
And I will dwell in the house
of the LORD forever.**

As we've seen, the 23rd Psalm is an overview of how God takes care of his sheep. Jesus described himself in John 10 as the "Good Shepherd." In the same passage, he referred to his followers as "his sheep." Psalm 23 is David's testimonial as to how the Good Shepherd, the risen Lord Jesus, cares for his sheep.

The summary statement of David's testimonial is found in verse 1, where David says, "The Lord *is* my shepherd; I shall not want." In other words, as God's sheep, God has promised to give us everything we'll ever need to make it through this life. The rest of the psalm is merely an enumeration, an amplification, an expansion upon this one great truth.

Before we look at the concluding verse of the psalm, let's remind ourselves of what God has already promised us in the preceding verses. As an outworking of God's commitment to provide all our needs as his sheep, our heavenly shepherd has promised us:

1. Spiritual refreshment and strength (verses 2–3)— "He makes me to lie down in green pastures; He leads me beside the still waters. He restores my soul."

2. Divine guidance (verse 3)—"He leads me in the paths of righteousness for His name's sake."

3. God's reassuring presence with us (verse 4)— "Yea, though I walk through the valley of the shadow of death, I will fear no evil; for You *are* with me."

4. God's powerful protection (verse 4)—"Your rod and Your staff, they comfort me."

5. God's advance planning for our lives (verse 5)— "You prepare a table before me in the presence of my enemies; You anoint my head with oil."

6. God's abundant generosity and beneficence (verse 5) —"My cup runs over."

Now, here in verse 6 looking ahead to the future, both in this world and the next. He says, "Surely goodness and mercy shall follow me all the days of my life; and I will dwell in the house of the LORD forever."

David makes a transition from what God has done for his sheep in the past to the assurance that God gives his sheep for the future. My friend, no matter where you and I may be as one of God's sheep, whether we're kind of relaxed or whether we're facing a deep crisis, we need these words of assurance. We need to hear God reassure us that up ahead, in the misty future, he has put everything in place for us to enjoy earthly blessing and eternal security.

I've known this verse since I was a child. I've recited it out loud more times than I can remember. But I don't think I ever fully appreciated what God was saying to me in this verse until now.

First, look at God's promise here of earthly blessing.
"Surely goodness and mercy shall follow me all the days of
my life."

Goodness and mercy—this is what God promises us
all the days of our life. Whatever may come, I can be
sure that God's goodness and mercy will always be in
the picture. Whatever I do, I am assured that God will
always treat me with goodness and mercy.

"Goodness" means God's blessing. It means God's
bounty and munificence.

"Mercy" means God's forgiveness, kindness and
compassion. It means God's forbearance and
graciousness even when my performance doesn't deserve
such treatment.

Goodness supplies all my needs while mercy blots
out all my failures and sins. And here in Psalm 23, God
promises us that, as his sheep, both of these great
spiritual commodities will accompany us in our walk
through this life.

The Hebrew word here translated "follow" literally
means "to tag along right behind somebody." David is
declaring that wherever we go, whether we turn left or
right, whether we go up or down, God's goodness and
mercy are permanently along for the ride.

It's like being on a roller coaster. Wherever the first
car goes, the following cars are hooked up to it. And as
God's sheep, the Bible says that God's goodness and
mercy are hooked up to us just like that. Wherever our
car goes, their car is going as well.

And the Bible says that this roller-coaster connection
will remain true "all the days of our life." Not just in the
bright days but in the dark days too. Not just in the days
of feasting but in the days of ashes and mourning also.

Not just in the cheery days of summer but in the dreary
days of winter as well. Through it *all*, God promises that
we will continually experience his goodness and mercy.

Now how can God make a promise like this? How can
he back it up? How can he be so certain that goodness
and mercy will appear in every situation of our life?

Well, the answer is because of something we saw
earlier in this psalm. In verse 4, God said that he would
be with us as his sheep wherever we go. Jesus said in
Hebrews 13:5, "I WILL NEVER DESERT YOU, NOR WILL I EVER
FORSAKE YOU." Everywhere I go, all the days of my life,
God promises that he is going there with me. This means
that his *character* and his *nature* are going with me
wherever I go in life.

And this, you see, is the secret. God's *character* is
always merciful. God's *nature* is always to treat his sheep
with goodness. As long as we have God's character and
nature with us, we can never experience *anything
different* from who and what God is. And God is good
and God is merciful.

Now it's important we understand that this (that is,
goodness and mercy) is not the way God *acts*, it's simply
the way he *is*. And therefore, by definition, anyone who
has God as an integral part of his life must become the
recipient of these character traits that mark his every
deed and thought.

Years ago, when my oldest son, James, was nine
years old, and I dropped him off for a week of baseball
camp, I said to him as I prepared to leave, "Now,
Jamie, Mom and I aren't going to be here with you.
Probably no one else you know is going to be here
with you. But Jesus promised that he would be here
with you. So if you need something, ask him for a
good answer, because he always treats his followers

with goodness. If you mess up or find yourself in
trouble, ask him for mercy, because he always treats
his followers with mercy."

I went on to say, "You know, son, when I got sent off
to camp alone as a child, I didn't have this kind of
confidence. I wasn't a follower of Jesus Christ. I wasn't
one of God's personal sheep. I went off to camp feeling
totally alone and insecure because *nobody* was with me.
But that's not the case with you."

Now this is not just a truth for children going to
camp. It's also a truth for adults facing a scary world
every day. Everywhere you and I go as God's sheep,
Jesus is with us. Because *he* is with us, his character
and his nature are with us. And because God's
character and nature are always goodness and mercy,
this is what we can be assured of receiving in every
circumstance of life. God simply cannot treat his sheep
any other way—it would be a violation of his very
character and nature.

Listen to these Scriptures.

Psalm 25:8: "Good and upright is the LORD."

Psalm 31:19: "How great is Your goodness, which
You have stored up for those who fear You . . .
before the sons of men!"

Psalm 86:5: "For You, Lord, are good, and ready to
forgive, and abundant in lovingkindness to all who
call upon You."

Psalm 103:11: "For as high as the heavens are
above the earth, so great is His lovingkindness
toward those who fear Him."

Lamentations 3:22–23: "The LORD'S
lovingkindnesses indeed never cease, for His
compassions never fail. They are new every
morning; great is Your faithfulness."

I could go on citing verses for pages that tell us about
the goodness and mercy God has and shows to his sheep.
As I said earlier, this is not something God *does*. This is
simply the way God *is*. This is a most important point.
You see, if goodness and mercy were things that God *did*,
then at any point, God can make up his mind not to do
them anymore. But if goodness and mercy are things that
God *is*, then God can't stop doing them unless and until
he stops being God. And this is never going to happen.

Therefore, wherever we go, all the days of our life, God
is there with us, bringing his goodness and mercy with
him. This is why David can say with such utter confidence,
"Surely goodness and mercy *shall* follow me all the days of
my life," because *God* is going to follow with us all the
days of our lives. As long as God remains God, this is the
only way possible for him to treat his sheep.

I recently sat in my study and began thinking back on
how many jams I've gotten myself into over the years.
Sometimes it was my job performance that got me in
them; sometimes it was my poor spending habits;
sometimes it was my arrogance or some other weakness
in my character; much of the time it was my big mouth!

I love to watch reruns of *The Honeymooners*, that
famous sitcom starring Jackie Gleason as Ralph Cramden.
In episode after episode, I watch as Ralph gets himself
into one jam after another. And almost without exception,
it's his arrogance and his big mouth that is responsible.
In fact, one of Gleason's most famous *schticks* is when
he would cry out with bulging eyes, "I've got a *biiiigggg*

mouth!" And I sit there in front of the TV and say to myself, "Hey, Ralphie boy, I know exactly how you feel."

A few years ago, a friend told me, "Lon, you step in more cow pies than any person I've ever met." And that friend was right!

And yet, here's the amazing part: somehow, when I turn to God and say, "Lord, I've gotten myself into a big mess again. It was my fault and I know it. But I'm asking you to please show me mercy and goodness in spite of myself"—it's amazing how God always extricates me from what looks like impending disaster. But should I really regard this as such an amazing thing? Isn't this exactly what God promised that he'd do for me as his sheep? We just have to humble ourselves, call on him and give him the chance.

Now if you're in a deep and dark valley in your life, you're probably thinking, "Oh yeah, well there's no goodness and mercy from God where I am right now. As I look around, frankly, all I see is disaster and catastrophe."

Please allow me to suggest that we often feel this way because we define God's expressions of "goodness and mercy" in a far too limited way. In other words, God's "goodness" doesn't always and only mean human health, wealth and prosperity. God's "mercy" doesn't always and only mean complete deliverance from anything we dislike.

We must learn to see God's workings in a deeper way. Sometimes God's "goodness and mercy" means God is taking us to places we don't want to go and giving us things we don't want to have—as part of his larger plan for our spiritual growth and development into men and women of God. If we miss this, we will often end up accusing God and impugning him when, in reality, he's actually doing exactly what he said he would. It's just that, in our limited perspective as human beings, we aren't able to recognize it yet.

I got a letter from a lady a while back whom I had never met. Someone had passed on to her a tape series I did called "Brokenness" while she was quite ill and confined to bed. In this letter, she said that as she was lying on her sickbed, she felt as though the Lord had forsaken her and forgotten about her. She said that she had bottomed out with bitterness, anger and resentment. And then those tapes came. She said she listened to those tapes as I explained how God, in his great love for us, uses sickness and illness to break our pride and self-reliance. This lady said she had to write and tell me how those tapes had radically transformed her outlook on her circumstances.

She said, "I lay here now and I thank God, because I can see his goodness and his mercy operating in my situation like I couldn't before." She went on to explain that she had been so caught up in defining God's goodness and mercy in terms of money and success and health and mobility that she had failed to understand that this is not always the form in which God sends his blessings. And now that she was liberated from such a narrow definition, she was suddenly able to see goodness and mercy in her circumstances that she had never seen before.

When Brenda and I were at our lowest point with our daughter's illness, we felt the way this lady did. We looked around and couldn't see anything but devastation and bleakness. It was impossible to see how "goodness and mercy" applied to our situation at all.

But we remembered what God told Isaiah: "'For My thoughts are not your thoughts, nor are your ways My ways,' declares the Lord. 'For as the heavens are higher than the earth, so are My ways higher than your ways and My thoughts than your thoughts'" (Isaiah 55:8–9). In light of this verse, we decided to believe God and actively look for his mercy and goodness in our circumstances. And when we looked, we found it.

Yes, our daughter was suffering and we were exhausted. But our other three boys were healthy and doing well. Our marriage was stronger than it had ever been. God was blessing my ministry in extraordinary ways at McLean Bible Church. People were praying for us faithfully. God was meeting all our financial needs in spite of Jill's medical expenses. Our church family had begun a ministry to help children with disabilities and their families as a result of watching our struggle. This ministry, called ACCESS Ministry today, has gone on to develop into the largest targeted ministry to children with disabilities in any local church in America that we know of. Honestly, there was goodness and mercy all around us. All we had to do was open our eyes and see it.

As you read all of this, maybe you're going through some tough times and you feel the way this lady said she felt: bottomed out with bitterness. Maybe you feel like Brenda and I did: unable to see anything but devastation and bleakness. Well, I'd like to say to you that if you're one of God's sheep, I can assure you that there is goodness and mercy all around you, if you will only rise above your pain and look for it.

At every crossroads, at every crisis, at every catastrophe, at every critical moment in our lives, there is goodness and mercy, because God promises it will be there. There is goodness and mercy in every place where God takes us, because that's the way God is and that's the only way he leads. We must simply step back and allow God to show us where his goodness and mercy are operating even in the midst of our pain and suffering.

Second, when we leave this life and we no longer

**need any goodness or mercy here on earth, God has
a promise for us there too.** "I will dwell in the house of
the LORD forever."

Now "the house of the Lord" is merely a synonym for
heaven. It's symbolic of where God is, where God lives.
So what God is promising us is an eternal domicile, an
eternal residence, in his heavenly dwelling. We will be
God's permanent houseguests there for all eternity. As
God's sheep, I don't ever have to leave his sheepfold.
This is what the Bible says: I'm a member of God's flock
"forever." Forever!

How long exactly is forever? Well, I don't know for
sure. It's way beyond my finite ability to comprehend it.
But however long it is, that's how long I'm welcomed in
the house of God. Folks, God makes no bogus
promises. If God says "forever," he means "forever."
Jesus said, "In My Father's house are many dwelling
places; if it were not so, I would have told you; for I go
to prepare a place for you. If I go and prepare a place
for you, I will come again and receive you to Myself,
that where I am, there you may be also" (John 14:2–3).

In Galatians 4:5, 7, Paul says that we have received
"the adoption as sons. . . . Therefore, you are no longer
a slave, but a son." The Bible declares believers in Jesus
Christ to be God's "children" in a way the rest of the
human race isn't. And as Jesus said in John 8:35, "The
slave does not remain in the house forever; the son does
remain forever." And because we are God's children, this
is the birthright we have.

In 1 Thessalonians 4:16–17, Paul tells us that the Lord
Jesus will return to the earth "with a shout, with the
voice of the archangel and with the trumpet of God, and
the dead in Christ will rise first. Then we who are alive
and remain will be caught up together with them in the

clouds to meet the Lord in the air." Many people stop here and miss the very best part of the verse. It concludes with these words: "and so we shall *always* be with the Lord." It doesn't really matter whether the Lord's return is pre-trib, mid-trib or post-trib. It doesn't matter if it's pre-mil, a-mil or post-mil. Whenever it comes, the key point is, "and so we shall *always* be with the Lord." We are *permanent* members of God's household.

No one in the universe can change this—not even the Devil himself. That's why Jesus said, "My sheep hear My voice, and I know them, and they follow Me; and I give eternal life to them, and they will never perish; and no one will snatch them out of My hand. My Father, who has given them to Me, is greater than all; and no one is able to snatch them out of the Father's hand" (John 10:27–29).

Now, until someone comes along who's greater than God himself, this promise Jesus made his sheep is absolutely secure. And I might add, no one is ever going to come along who is powerful enough to rob God of his sheep. So this is our promise, our eternal promise. God made it and God means it. *And we can take this to the bank.*

When my youngest son, Jonathan, was two years old, we were deeply involved in trying to teach him the rules of our house. We had learned from our older two sons that the best way to teach little people is to let them repeat after you. We basically drilled things into their heads through rote memorization.

One of the things I was trying to drill into this little boy was that "when I say no, I mean no." Finally I got him to the place where I would say to him, "Johnny, when Daddy says no, Daddy what?" and he would look back at me and say, "Daddy mean no!" And I'd say, "That's exactly right, son. Here's a cookie!" Seriously, that's the way we work in our house. For the effective functioning of a family, it's essential that a good father establish this from the beginning: when Daddy says no, he means what he says.

Now God's the best father who's ever lived. And when God says no, he means no. But, and here's the great news, when God says yes, God means yes! When God looks at the rest of our lives as his sheep, God says yes to goodness and mercy. And when God looks forward to eternity for us, God says yes to heaven and eternal life for us. God means what he says and **we can depend on it!**

I want to close with the words of a man who believed that when God said yes, God meant yes. He is one of the people I am most looking forward to meeting when I get to heaven. His name was Dwight L. Moody. Moody was the greatest American evangelist of the 19th century—the Billy Graham of the 19th century, if you will. And he wrote these words:

> Someday you will read in the papers that D. L. Moody of East Northfield is dead. Don't you believe a word of it! At that moment I shall be more alive than I am now; I shall have gone up higher, that is all, out of this old clay tenement into a house that is immortal—a body that death cannot touch, that sin cannot taint; a body fashioned like unto His glorious body. I was born of the flesh in 1837. I was born of the Spirit in 1856. That which is born of the flesh may die. That which is born of the Spirit will live forever.[12]

This is the kind of certainty and assurance that God wants to give every one of us as his sheep. So believe him. There's no reason not to.

Father, the Word of God is precious to us, because it teaches us about your character, your nature and your promises. We rejoice in those things because we know that they cannot change. We realize that when you open a door, no man can shut it. We realize that when you say yes, no being in the universe can say no.

And so, thank you, Lord, that you have said yes to so many things here in Psalm 23. You've said yes to meeting our every need and giving us spiritual refreshment and divine guidance. You've said yes to always being with us and protecting us with your awesome power. You've said yes to planning our lives out in advance in such a way that "our cup runs over."

And now you end by telling us yes, wherever we go in life, there will be goodness and mercy. And when it's all over, yes, we will dwell in the house of the Lord forever.

Thank you that one of these days all of your sheep will know what it feels like to step onto the shores of heaven, to breathe celestial air and to see Jesus face-to-face. At that moment, we will marvel that it ever even crossed our minds to doubt and question your promises.

And so, Father, I pray that you will help us believe what you tell us in the Bible and trust you. I especially pray for folks who are struggling with areas of their life where, from their perspective, they don't see any goodness or mercy. God, I pray that you would change the way they look at their circumstances, that you would change their perspective from that of this world to that of Almighty God. Help them see, Lord, that you have put them in a place where goodness and mercy abound, if they will only let you open their eyes so they can see it.

And finally, Father, we thank you that your goodness and mercy toward us extend into eternity—

*that they don't end at the grave but that they are going
to last forever.*

*Lord, you're a great God. And the greatest thing about
you is that you love folks like us. Thank you for that.
Thank you for agreeing to be our heavenly shepherd. And
thank you for your promises, which can never fail.*

May we believe them and trust you.

In Jesus' name. Amen.

Endnotes

1. Henry Ward Beecher, *Life Thoughts, Gathered from the
Extemporaneous Discourses of Henry Ward Beecher* (Boston: Phillips,
Sampson and Company, 1859), p. 9.

2. Frederick William Robertson, *Sermons Preached at Brighton* (New
York: Harper & Brothers, 1873), pp. 405–6.

3. R. Kelso Carter, "Standing on the Promises," 1886.

4. Cleland B. McAfee, "Near to the Heart of God," 1903.

5. Annie Johnson Flint, "He Giveth More Grace," c. 1941, renewal 1969
by Lillenas Publishing Co.

6. Horatio G. Spafford and Phillip P. Bliss, "It Is Well with My Soul,"
1876.

7. Sidney Cox, "My Lord Knows the Way Through the Wilderness," c.
1951, renewal 1979, Singspiration Music.

8. Robert Robinson, "Come Thou Fount of Every Blessing," 1759.

9. W. Phillip Keller, *A Shepherd Looks at Psalm 23* (Grand Rapids:
Zondervan, 1970), pp. 100–101.

10. Thomas Chisholm and William Runyan, "Great Is Thy Faithfulness,"
c. 1923, renewal 1951, Hope Publishing.

11. Joachin Neander, 1680; translated by Catherine Winkworth, "Praise
Ye the Lord, the Almighty," 1863.

12. Dwight L. Moody, http://www.swordofthelord.com/biographies/
MoodyDL.htm.

A LOST SHEEP FROM THE HOUSE OF ISRAEL COMES HOME

It has been said that if you are Jewish, you can only grow up to be one of three things: a doctor, a lawyer or a failure. Guess what? By that definition I fall into the final category. You see, my story is about how a nice Jewish boy from Portsmouth, Virginia, ended up as the pastor of a big evangelical church in McLean, Virginia. A Jewish pastor might sound strange, but then again, my story could read as a Hollywood screenplay.

I was born and raised in Portsmouth, Virginia, by Conservative Jewish parents. My dad grew up in a very religious home; my mom did not. My dad's parents were from the "old country" (Europe). My grandfather was from Romania and my grandmother from Germany. According to family lore, they met as teenagers on the boat coming to America, fell in love and got married. My dad's parents were strongly Orthodox. I remember as a young child watching my grandmother prepare the *Shabbat* (Sabbath) meal before sundown each Friday. My grandparents left all the light switches on in their home so as not to violate the rabbinic rules about "lighting a fire" on the Sabbath. They walked to the synagogue instead of driving, an activity prohibited on the Sabbath.

My parents were not nearly as religious. Like many others, they saw religion as an obligation and not a way to know God personally. We never had a Bible in our home. We did not sit down and pray together before meals; in fact we didn't pray at all. We lit candles every Sabbath, went to the High Holiday services at *Rosh Hashanah* and *Yom Kippur*, and had a Passover *seder* meal in our home. But the presence of God was not a reality in our lives.

We attended Congregation *Gomley Chesed*, the largest Conservative synagogue in Portsmouth. Most of the Jewish people in Portsmouth were members; hundreds of families attended. With its own country club, the affluent Portsmouth Jewish community was very insular. But that was not necessarily our choice. My mother explained that Jewish people were not allowed in the Gentile country club, so we started our own. We were members of the club and went there often. The synagogue, the neighborhood, the country club—our relationships and friends were all in that community. I did not really have any Gentile friends until I got to high school.

On Yom Kippur my dad would fast, and I would do my best. As a child I found the story of the Day of Atonement very intimidating. I was terrified by the idea that God was seated up in heaven with an eternal ledger called the Book of Life that included all the names of those who go to heaven, and that at the end of Yom Kippur, he would close the Book for the year. I imagined God as a big grandfather with a long beard and a

Gutenberg Bible. I will never forget when I was about nine or ten, coming out of synagogue at the end of Yom Kippur with my dad. I asked him, "Dad, how do you know if your name is written in the Book of Life for the next year?" He thought for a minute and said, "Well, I guess if you live until next Yom Kippur, you know your name was in there." That was his answer and he was completely serious. I remember thinking, *Oh my gosh! What kind of assurance is this?* It struck me even as a child, *Is this all we've got to hold on to? I mean, this is nothing to hold on to!* I was looking for something and my dad, whom I thought was the greatest, couldn't offer me anything.

I grew up believing that God probably existed, but not knowing anything about him. I would sometimes lie in bed and try to talk to him. But I never felt any real connection with him.

I had my first experience of anti-Semitism when I was ten. I was away at summer camp when some of the other campers started calling me names such as "Jew boy." The ugly scene happened when I was so young that I soon pushed it out of my mind. But if any anti-Semitism existed in Portsmouth, I never saw it.

I went to Hebrew school twice a week after public school, leading up to my *bar mitzvah* at age thirteen. I also went to Sunday school at the synagogue because my father went to the men's group every Sunday morning. In Sunday school we read books about the history of the Jews and learned Bible stories. Once I was bar mitzvah, I gradually stopped going to Hebrew school and Sunday school. For my bar mitzvah I read a passage from Isaiah that I had studied for about a year. I was good at reading Hebrew, so after my bar mitzvah I was given the honor of reading the Torah and blessings in the weekly services. I continued doing this for a year—not because I felt connected to the synagogue but because I felt it was expected of me as a good Jewish boy.

When I entered high school, my previously steady relationship with the synagogue changed. The distractions of teenage life, such as girls, partying and drinking were much more fun than synagogue. I enjoyed being a member of my school's Thespian troupe. During play practice, we would sit around and chat if we were not onstage. One day, one of the girls in the play started asking me questions about my "personal relationship" with God and if I was sure if I was going to heaven. I'd never heard of a personal relationship with God or thought or talked much about heaven. It was never mentioned at home or in the synagogue, so I saw no connection between heaven and my Judaism. If anything, I thought being Jewish fast-tracked me into heaven. However, this girl's incessant questioning left me wondering.

I stored up questions for the rabbi. When I saw him I asked, "Do Jews go to heaven or hell?" I thought he was going to have a coronary! He looked at me as if to say, "What kind of question is that?" I explained what my friend at school had asked. He said, "All Jews go to heaven." I replied, "That's wonderful. How can I defend myself against this girl?" The rabbi said, "Just tell her that we are all Abraham's descendants and so we have a different arrangement with God than the rest of the world. We are the Chosen People."

I said, "You mean I could do almost anything I want and still go to heaven because I am Jewish?" He said, "Yes, that's basically it." I thought to myself, *Wow! So even if I never go to synagogue again, I am still going to heaven.* That pretty well ended my relationship with the synagogue! And from the age of fifteen until I began to search for meaning in the later years of college, it never once crossed my mind that I wasn't going to heaven.

Years later when I was studying the *Mishnah* (Jewish rabbinical writings) as part of my graduate work at Johns Hopkins University, I found a passage that strongly implies that all Jewish people (with a handful of exceptions) are going to heaven. This interpretation from Sanhedrin Tractate 90a is based on Isaiah 60:21, which states, "Then all your people will be righteous; they will possess the land forever." The point is that what my rabbi was saying back then was not just some wild opinion he had invented on his own but was actually based on rabbinical teaching.

I reached age eighteen and, confident I was going to heaven, headed off to the University of North Carolina at Chapel Hill. Like most college students, I relished the freedom of not being under my parents' roof. I joined a social fraternity that made the one in the movie *Animal House* look like a religious day school. I got deeply involved in drinking, partying, women and gambling. We would gamble from four o'clock in the afternoon through the night, then wake up and eat lunch and at about four o'clock start again. I almost never went to class. I was there for fun! All a person had to do was maintain a 2.0 grade point average and everything was fine.

But by my junior year that lifestyle was starting to get stale. A lot of things that had started out very exciting began to wear out. After a while, getting drunk one more time or having one more woman was not very fulfilling. What's more, I had begun to think a little more seriously about the issues of life. "Where am I going?" "What is my life all about?" "What am I doing here?" Those questions were beginning to plague me and I did not have any answers.

When I began college in 1966, the Vietnam War was heating up, but it was so far away from me that I didn't really care. When I became a junior, that changed. Realizing that I would soon be leaving college and might

get drafted to go to Vietnam led me to become politically
active. I marched in Washington, D.C., and other places
against the war.

At the same time, I got involved in the drug culture
and the hippie movement. When a fraternity brother
invited me to smoke dope with him and some friends, I
jumped at the chance. I had smoked cigarettes for years,
so inhaling wasn't new to me. As I continued to puff and
got high, I thought, *Wow, this is something totally different!*

I spent the summer of 1969 in the "Borscht Belt"
(Jewish resort area) in the Catskill Mountains in New
York. I hitchhiked there with some friends, and we found
jobs in a restaurant hotel. Toward the end of that
summer, some friends of mine said, "Hey, we need to go
to Woodstock." My friends explained to me that it was a
music festival and I thought it sounded pretty wonderful.
In fact, I may be one of the few people in the world that
actually bought a ticket to Woodstock. They expected
only 50,000 people, and when 500,000 showed up, no
one worried about tickets. Still, I can only imagine how
much my ticket stub would be worth today if I'd kept it.

I'd dabbled in drugs in Chapel Hill, but it was in New
York that summer that I first took LSD. My friends said, "If
you are looking for answers to questions about the universe,
you need to take this stuff. It will expand your mind."

I went back to college that fall convinced that I had
found the pathway to enlightenment. I had become a
very strong advocate of drugs. Of the men in my
fraternity who ended up using drugs, I introduced over
half of them to that world and provided the drugs to start
them on their way. We did drugs all the time. I grew my
hair out to my shoulders in an Afro. My hair does not
grow down. It grows out! I wore bell-bottoms, a tank
top, love beads and motorcycle boots and really looked
the part. The nice thing about hair like that is I could

hide joints behind my ears, and pull my hair over them and hide them from the police. I would start the day with four joints behind each ear, and as the day progressed we would smoke them. We dropped LSD four or five times a week. It was much more fun to sit up in a tree and smoke dope than it was to go to class. In fact, there is a picture on the inside cover of my college yearbook of me and several fraternity brothers sitting in a tree in the middle of campus smoking dope!

I may be the only person in the history of the University of North Carolina who flunked honors chemistry. I got into the class because my earlier marks as an undergraduate were good enough, but then I never went to class. It was well known that all you had to do to get an A was show up. At the end of the semester, the professor gave me an F. I thought, *How dare he give me an F!* I pleaded with him for a D and he said, "Are you kidding? You were never here!"

This forced me to remain at Chapel Hill for a fifth year in order to graduate. It was during this fifth year (my "victory lap," as we used to call it!) that my entire life changed. But more on that in a moment.

I became well known in Chapel Hill as a dope pusher. My friends and I would travel to New York City and buy large shipments of dope, cut it and sell it. A friend even went to Amsterdam several times a year to bring back large amounts of hashish, which he would sew into the inside lining of his overcoat. These were the days before they had dogs and modern equipment to detect the drugs. Actually, I put myself through the last two years of college selling dope. I saw no point in getting a job when I could make more money and make it more easily selling dope. I generally had a big block of hashish sitting on my desk in my room. I had a balance scale that I had stolen from the chemistry department so that we could weigh the hash after we cut it.

One morning there was a knock at the door. It was the police. They yelled, "We have a warrant for the arrest of Lon Solomon on dope charges!" My friend was sleeping in the living room and there was dope everywhere. I looked out the window of my bedroom to see if I could jump. Although we were on the second floor, it wasn't that high. But the house was surrounded with police dogs. I was dead to rights. My friend answered the door and had the presence of mind to ask if he could see the search warrant. It turned out that somehow the police had a search warrant for the house next door. My friend told them they could not come in. If they had, I would have gone to jail! The police went to our friends' house next door, found the dope I had sold them, then went to class and arrested them.

All the time I was doing drugs, I thought I was making spiritual progress. I thought that I was moving forward toward a place where I would find the answers to the universe. But a real turning point came in 1971 (during my "victory lap" year). I was sitting on a wall with a friend, on the edge of campus at two o'clock in the morning, tripped out on LSD. I said, "You know, something is really bothering me. Here we are, the flower people, doing all these drugs. But instead of getting more loving and more caring, I really feel like I'm getting worse!" He turned to me and said, "Maybe you're just getting more honest about what you have been all along."

It was only a passing comment to him, but to me it felt like I'd been hit with a sledgehammer! I had grown up believing my own PR: that I was a good, kind, unselfish person. I believed I was destined for heaven; that's what my rabbi told me. Suddenly, I was faced with the prospect that all this wasn't true, that I had been deceiving myself—that I was a self-centered, unethical person in desperate need of help. As drugs became passé, I realized they couldn't change me from the inside out. I decided I needed religion. The more I thought about my friend's comment, the more I became convinced he was right. I realized I needed radical change. But I also realized that drugs were not the answer.

At first I was drawn to Eastern religions and read books on Zen Buddhism, Taoism and Confucianism. They all sounded wonderful on paper, but I couldn't make them work in real life. I would sit in the woods with my legs crossed for three hours, reading books on Zen Buddhism. But then I would just get hungry, go find my friends and ask, "Hey, what's for lunch?" Suddenly all my Zen was gone! I wasn't one bit different after three hours in the woods. Next, I wanted to put my hair into a ponytail and dance around on the street with the Hare Krishnas, except I hated their food! So I gave up on being a Hare Krishna.

Finally, I decided I wasn't an Eastern religion kind of person and maybe I needed to go back to Judaism. I had this sense of destiny, that somehow my life was headed into the spiritual realm. Maybe Orthodox Judaism had the answer. In fact, I began to think I should become a rabbi. I thought that perhaps if I were a rabbi, I would get the answers to the questions of the universe and figure it all out. So I went to see the campus rabbi. I sat down with my bell-bottoms and crazy hair and said, "I think God wants me to be a rabbi." He looked at me and said, "I don't think so." I shared with him the hunger I had in my heart and my spiritual need. He was clueless. All he did was give me a couple of books to read. I didn't want books! I wanted someone who could sit down, look me in the eye and say, "Lon, I know the answers to the questions you're asking. I know how you can get changed on the inside, and not be the ugly

person you know you are. I can help you." The rabbi
didn't do that, and I don't think he had any idea how to
meet my needs. I walked out of his office, thinking, *Man,
there's nothing here for me.*

Suddenly I felt lost. I always thought that, if all else
fails, I could go back to Judaism. But now that too was
gone. So I became desperate. I was really driven and
passionate about finding meaning in life. I didn't go to
class. I wasn't interested in gambling, partying or girls
any longer. I was driven by the idea that I had to find
out who I was, what I was doing here and what was
going to happen to me after I died. It was a really tough
year because no matter where I looked (including my
LSD trips), I couldn't find any answers that worked.

I became obsessed with finding the resources I needed
to live a meaningful life and to make me into the kind of
person I wanted to be. I'd sit around smoking dope with
my fraternity brothers and say, "Why are we here on
earth? What is our purpose? What is the meaning of life?"
They could not understand why I had all these questions.
Why couldn't I just be a normal person who graduates
from college, gets a job, gets married, raises kids, becomes
a grandfather and dies? My friends thought I had lost my
mind. Frankly, I began to wonder myself. I had heard
about guys who tripped out on LSD and never came back.
I started to panic that maybe I was on one of those trips.
*Maybe I will never come back. Maybe I'm in some
psychiatric hospital undergoing shock therapy, thinking
that I'm an orange and hiding under the bed or something.*

I didn't know what reality was anymore. I even began
to think about suicide. I hated the person I was on the
inside and now I was planning to take my own life. I
really planned on doing it, but since I procrastinated
on everything else in life in those days, I also put off
my suicide!

Then one day, in the spring of 1971, my life changed. I was walking down the streets of Chapel Hill with my German Shepherd, Noah. He got in a dogfight, right in front of the weirdest man in the universe. Bob Eckhardt was a man in his forties who worked in Durham and lived about eight miles from Chapel Hill. Every Saturday he would come into town with his wife in a white Econoline van with Scripture verses printed on the sides. Two megaphone speakers were mounted on the roof of his van so he could play hymns as he drove down the street. He became a regular fixture on the street corner of Chapel Hill handing out pamphlets about Jesus.

People spat on him, threw the tracts back at him and cursed him out. Week after week, I saw him and avoided him. But the day my dog got into a fight right in front of where Bob was standing, he helped me pull my dog off the little dog he was mangling. So here I am, eyeball to eyeball with the weirdest man in the world. What do you say to the weirdest man in the world? I looked at him and said, "Hi!" He said, "Hello!" *Now what should I say?* So I said, "Gotta go," and he said, "Okay, see you," and off I went! The whole encounter lasted no more than thirty seconds. But in those thirty seconds, face-to-face with this man, something inside of me said, *Lon, this guy has what you are looking for—the peace, the contentment, the wholeness, the healthiness.* I didn't have any empirical evidence that I could put in a test tube to prove it. I just knew it.

That gave me hope. You see, until I met Bob, I'd begun to think there weren't any answers for the questions I was asking. So for the next few weeks, I'd wander by him and take his pamphlets. I never talked with him. I was too scared! I developed quite a pile of religious pamphlets on my dresser, but I didn't read them. I took them because I felt sorry for him. He was a sincere guy and people were treating him nastily. Sincerity was at a premium in those days in Chapel Hill, and I figured that someone ought to be nice to Bob and at least take what he was handing out. I really wanted to talk to him. I just could not get up the nerve to do it.

Finally, one Saturday morning I walked up to him and said, "Hey, I umm, would like to come talk to you sometime." And he said, "Well, that would be wonderful. How about three o'clock this afternoon?"

Now I wasn't ready for that! It's kind of like when you go up to somebody in church and say, "Why don't you come over for lunch sometime?" and they respond, "Fine, how about today?" That's not what you meant! I expected him to say, "Okay, how about in a month or so?" giving me time to work up enough courage for the actual meeting.

So I replied, "You know what? I'm busy today, I've got another appointment." Now, what kind of appointment would a hippie have at three o'clock on a Saturday afternoon in Chapel Hill, North Carolina? I was lying through my teeth. But I was scared! I mumbled to him, "I gotta go, gotta go. Maybe some other time. We'll talk another time."

I started walking down the street with my dog and I got about ten yards. Bob cupped his hands around his mouth and screamed, "You may not be here next week!" I thought, *Oh my goodness.* It was a sunny spring day in Chapel Hill, and the streets were packed with students. I looked around trying to pretend that I didn't know whom he was addressing. *I don't want all these people knowing the weirdest man in the world is yelling at* me! So I hurried down the street, ducked around the corner, leaned up against the brick wall and thought, *Arggh! That was the worst experience of my whole life. I can't believe I did that!* But as I began walking around that day, I realized, *That guy is right. I have no guarantee I'll be here next week.* I had already lost several high school friends. I thought, *I should go talk to him.* So at three o'clock I showed up. He was gone!

I began to despair. I felt that this guy had given a prophecy that I was not going to live for another week! I was terrified that he had predicted my death. The next week was horrible. I became consumed with fear. A good friend of mine owned a motorcycle that he regularly let me ride—I did not ride it that week! I did not walk under ladders and God help me if a black cat walked in front of me!

The week finally passed, and that Saturday I got up at the crack of dawn, which in those days was about ten o'clock in the morning! I went downtown to see this guy. I don't know what would have happened if he hadn't come to town that day, but faithful as ever, about 10:30 he rolled into town in the white Econoline circus van. I walked over to him and told him, "Because of you, I've just lived the worse week of my life. We need to talk. There's got to be some sales pitch that goes with this thing that you do here, and I'm willing to listen."

Now I need to add that during my traumatic week I was so scared I thought I should get a Bible, primarily as a good luck charm. None of my friends had one. As you can imagine, owning a Bible did not really fit with our lifestyle. So I ventured out to the bookstore to buy one. I couldn't believe how expensive they were! We were between dope shipments and five dollars was all I had to my name. I made ends meet in creative ways. I had a deal with my fraternity house that if I served dinner as a waiter in the dining room, I got the leftovers. I had a lot of broccoli and cauliflower but not much steak! That was how I was surviving.

The cheapest Bible I could find was three dollars. I

grudgingly got in line to pay for it. My friend who had earlier suggested to me, "Maybe you're just getting more honest with yourself," came by and asked what I was doing. I said, "I'm buying a Bible." "What in the world are you doing that for?" he asked. I described the kind of week I was having, and he said, "Lon, now stop for a second. Think. If this God that you're worried about is so real, don't you think he could give you a Bible without you having to spend half of your life savings on it?" I thought, *Yeah, that sounds spiritual, that sounds good.* So I put the Bible back.

Now as I was talking with Bob Eckhardt that very next Saturday, he took out a Bible and started reading from both the Hebrew Scriptures and the New Testament. He began telling me Bible stories, some that I was familiar with and others I'd never heard. He read to me about Elijah and the prophets of Baal on Mount Carmel. I thought that was the greatest story I'd ever heard! We talked for about two hours and it was like water on a dry sponge. Then he said to me, "Okay, now are you ready to receive Jesus?"

"Excuse me?" I said in astonishment.

"Are you ready to receive Jesus?" he repeated.

Well, I had no idea what that meant.

"No," I replied. "It has been fun talking to you man, and this has been wonderful. But I am Jewish! Jewish people don't do this."

"Well, Jesus was Jewish," he said. "Do you realize that all the early followers of Jesus were Jewish? Everybody who wrote the Bible, with the exception of Luke, was Jewish."

"Nah, come on!"

"Did you know Peter was Jewish?"

"You've got to be kidding!" I figured he was a white Aryan WASP, and, of course, a Gentile. I said, "Well, Peter doesn't have to go face my parents. No, I don't really think so."

"Will you do me one favor?"

"Maybe."

"Will you promise me that you will at least read the Bible and let God have the chance to speak to you?"

"Well, yeah, I don't think it would do any harm to read from the Bible."

"Do you have a Bible?"

"Uh, no."

"Come here a second." Bob waved me over and opened the back of his van, and there was a huge box of brand-new Bibles! Cellophane wrapping and all! He took one and said to me, "Here."

"I don't have any money, so I can't pay you for it."

"I don't want you to pay for it. If you promise me you'll read it, I'll give it to you."

Now, this was getting way too weird. On Wednesday I had challenged God to prove himself by giving me a Bible. Honestly, in the crowd I ran with, the odds of somebody giving me a Bible were less than zero. Now, four days later, this guy opens his trunk and hands me a brand-new Bible! So I took the Bible and said, "I gotta go." And I left.

As I walked away I remember thinking, *This is freaky. Could this really be true? Could Jesus really be the Messiah of Israel? Could I have really backed into the God of the universe here?*

I was still pretty skeptical, but I kept my promise. I took the Bible home and began reading a little every night before I went to bed. I didn't know where to read, so I started in the beginning of the book, with Adam and Eve. Like most people, I knew their names but had never read the whole story. It was incredible. When I got to the section where so-and-so begot so-and-so and so-and-so

Young Lon at two years old

Lon (left) with his mother, Hermoine, and Brian, his brother

Lon at his bar mitzvah

Lon in high school

Lon's parents, Hermoine and Irving

Lon's fraternity house at the University of North Carolina, Chapel Hill

Lon's fraternity photo

*Lon (center) in class at
Capital Bible Seminary*

. . . and later as a professor there

*Lon's family at his
graduation from
seminary, left to right:
Lon's grandparents,
Edward P. and Mildred
Levine; Lon's parents,
Irving and Hermoine;
Lon, Brenda and
Brenda's parents, Beatrice
and William Lowry*

*Brenda and Lon
pose with their
family after their
wedding, June 28,
1974. From top left:
Brenda, Lon, Brian
(Lon's brother) and
Brian's wife, Joan;
front: Poppa (Lon's
grandfather),
Bubba (Lon's
grandmother), Lon's
parents, Irving and
Hermoine*

Lon's young family visits the White
House, December 1987

The family at Bethany Beach, Delaware

Lon and his son Justin

Brenda and Lon with son
James at his graduation
from the U.S. Naval
Academy

Bill Lowry (Brenda's dad), Lon's son Jon
and Lon at a Johns Hopkins baseball game

James and Julia Solomon's wedding,
March 18, 2000

Lon snags a huge piece of chocolate
cake (his passion!) at Justin and
Kim's rehearsal dinner

Justin and Kim Solomon's wedding,
July 5, 2008

Jon and Kristin Solomon's
wedding, July 20, 2008

Brenda, Jill and Lon

*Brenda and Jill
out for a walk*

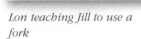

*Lon teaching Jill to use a
fork*

Brenda and Lon with grankids Tyler and Mia

Lon preaching at
McLean Bible Church

Lon leads a study tour to
Israel every year
(Photo by I Do Photography, Inc.)

Brenda and Lon with Dave
Dravecky, former pitcher for the
San Francisco Giants

Lon and Dr. James Dobson,
founder of Focus on the
Family

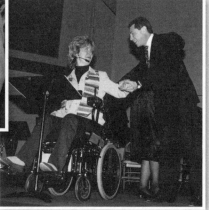

Joni Eareckson Tada with Lon at
McLean Bible Church

begot so-and-so, I decided to move on to the New
Testament because it talks about Jesus.

Now, I didn't know how the New Testament was
constructed, if it was a collection of short stories or an
anthology of poetry or whatever. I didn't know what the
thing was! So I figured you start at the beginning, right? I
turned to the Gospel of Matthew and started reading. I
could not believe some of the stuff that was in there! I
must have read the Sermon on the Mount seven or eight
times in a row before I could go on. I was impressed by
the way Jesus used words to cut right to the heart of the
matter. He could say more in one sentence than some of
my college professors could say in a whole semester (of
course, I wasn't in class much!). Then I reached Matthew
11 where Jesus says, "Come to Me, all you who labor
and are heavy-laden and overburdened, and I will cause
you to rest . . . you will find rest for your souls"
(Matthew 11:28–29 Amplified Version). It was as though
Jesus was speaking directly to me. This is exactly what I
had been looking for! I thought, *I've given drugs, Zen
Buddhism and Judaism a fair shot in my life. I gave
women, partying and drinking a go. It is only fair that I
give Jesus a chance. I just don't know how.* Bob had said,
"Receive Jesus." I didn't have one clue what that meant!
If he had said, "Stand on your head and spit nickels," I
would have at least known what position to be in! I
didn't have Bob's phone number, nor did I know another
born again follower of Jesus in the whole world, so I was
on my own.

I got down on my knees, because it just seemed
appropriate, and I prayed, "Okay God, I don't even know
if you are real and I'm really confused about this Jesus.
But I'm empty, scared and hurting and I need some help.
Jesus promises he can give me rest and joy. So God, I am
going to give you my life for one month. One month, and

I will go anywhere you want me to go, do anything you want me to do." I did not know how he was going to answer this prayer, but I was sincere. I said "If at the end of that month, God, you have not given me this joy and this rest, I reserve the right to take my life back and cancel the deal. But if you really give it to me, then you can have my life for good. A deal is a deal. Amen."

Now I realize that is probably one of the worst salvation prayers ever. I didn't know how to pray to God. I just had a sincere heart and wanted to do business with God. I figured a month ought to be long enough if he is God. I am so glad for the verse in the Bible that says "Man looks at the outward appearance, but the LORD looks at the heart" (1 Samuel 16:7). I am so glad that God up in heaven said, "Lon, that is the most awful prayer for salvation I've ever heard, but you know what? I'm going to look past that prayer and look at your heart. I see in your heart that you mean business. So I'm going to forget about the prayer and deal with your heart." I'm so relieved that God sees the heart!

I got up off my knees and I have to confess that I was very skeptical. I really didn't think this was going to work. Then it occurred to me, *I need more than this. I need some kind of authentication that God is real.* So I got back on my knees and said, "God, one more thing . . . my dog has the mange." Mange is when the fur starts falling off! I had been putting this salve on the dog that the vet had given me, but my dog was losing even more fur. So I said, "God, I am going to stop using the medicine on my dog because I want you to heal my dog." Then I got up and thought, *Maybe that's not a fair deal for the dog. Maybe I should have asked God to levitate the bed or something. But a prayer's a prayer. We'll see what happens.* I wanted a God who was at least powerful enough that he could handle a case of the mange!

Well, within three or four days, the mange had completely cleared up! You can explain it any way you want. But I knew it was not that medicine; I had been using the medicine on the dog and he had been getting worse. I knew what I had prayed and I knew God had done something for me.

God began doing some other things for me on the inside that I couldn't outwardly prove to anyone. But they were very real. The most compelling of them all was that God suddenly resuscitated my long-dormant conscience. All of a sudden, things I used to do and say that I would never have given a second thought to a week before— now, when I did those same things, I was overwhelmed with deep guilt and conviction about how wrong they were. I knew this new sensitivity to sin wasn't something I had done or invented. I knew that something supernatural had happened inside me—something that I had never experienced before—and I had no explanation for it except that God had entered my life.

A week later I got back down on my knees and said, "God, I am convinced. You have not only changed everything for my dog, but there are things changing inside me! There's a joy and a peace and a contentment that I've never felt before." And, as I said, there was also a sensitivity to sin that I never had before. There were things I used to be able to do without the slightest pang of conscience, and suddenly they were bothering me. The only way I could deal with them was when I asked God to forgive me, and then I'd feel fine. I'd never repented (or had the desire to) before. I knew I didn't create the changes that were going on inside of me. Something supernatural was happening.

So here I was, back on my knees, declaring, "God, I'm convinced! A deal's a deal. I told you I would give you my life for good. I don't know what you can do with a hippie whose hair is out to his shoulders and who blows dope, but whatever you can do with me, I give you my life for good." Soon after that I gave up selling and using drugs and have not touched them since.

The next time Bob Eckhardt came to town, I went up to him and told him the whole story. He grabbed me, hugged me and called his wife out of the back of the van, yelling, "Amy! Amy, you gotta come here quick and hear this!" He said, "Tell her, tell her!" So I told her the whole story. Full of joy, she said, "Praise the Lord!" and started dancing around. I'm looking at these people hugging each other and I'm thinking, *What in the world have I gotten myself into? I hope I am not going to act like this when I've been a Christian for a while!* (Bob later told me that in all the time he went to Chapel Hill every Saturday that spring and summer of 1971, as far as he knows, I am the only person who came to Jesus as a direct result of his being there. There may have been others whom we do not know about, but I like to think God sent Bob Eckhardt to Chapel Hill just for me.)

The next thing I knew, Bob was saying, "Lon, you need to get baptized."

"What?" I exclaimed. "I'm Jewish, man. Jewish people don't get baptized."

"Well, Jewish people don't believe in Jesus either, and you've already done that."

"Good point."

So I went home and began thinking about it. If I meant business here, I better really mean it. After all, you don't get half pregnant! You don't become half a Christian! I knew the Bible said that if you are serious about your relationship with Jesus, you need to be baptized. So I said, "Let's do it!" Bob baptized me in a pond in Chapel Hill.

Bob challenged me to go public. He got me out on

the streets, handing out tracts with him a week after I
became a Christian. It was a great way to begin my
Christian life. Then he said, "You need to go and tell
your parents." So I did. My parents weren't excited or
angry. They had a *laissez faire* attitude: "It's just another
fad. He has been into drugs, alcohol, being a hippie. If
we just leave him alone, he'll get over it."

There was one "family member" whom I knew would
not think it a fad and would actually be glad to hear
about my faith. She was an African-American lady named
Cora Lee Goodman. She was one of the most precious
women in my whole life. She came to work as a maid
for my family when I was two months old and worked
for my family all the way through the time I went away
to college. She was not an educated woman. She had
only finished the third grade. She couldn't write her own
name or read or drive a car. After I became a Christian, I
began hearing Christian songs. One of them was "Blessed
Assurance, Jesus Is Mine." I thought, *I've heard that song
somewhere before. But where? I knew they didn't sing it in
the synagogue!* Then it came back to me. I remembered,
when I was very little, Cora humming that tune and
others while she was ironing or fixing meals. I realized
she must be a Christian. So I hitchhiked up to
Portsmouth Virginia, to find her. She hadn't seen me for
three or four years, and I looked a lot different now with
my hippie hair and attire. I knocked on her door. She
pulled the curtains open, looked at me and drew back
the curtains. So I knocked again and she pulled open the
curtains again. I said, "Cora, let me in. It's Lonnie!" She
opened the door, still with the chain across.

Looking out, she said, "What are you doing here?"

"Cora, I've come here to tell you that I've given my
life to Jesus."

"Good God Almighty, honey! Come on in here!"

So we sat down and I told her the whole story. She told me, "Lon, I want you to know something. I've been praying for you and your family since I came to work for you when you were two months old. But honey, I *never* thought I'd see the day you become a Christian."

I said, "Well here I am." We had such a wonderful time together.

I told Cora Lee, "I think I'm gong to call my grandparents, and my aunt and uncle and tell them that I believe in Jesus."

"Lonnie, I'm not so sure that's a good idea."

"No, no, no Cora. By the time I get through explaining things to them, it will be as clear as the nose on my face."

"Honey, I just don't know if that's a good idea."

I called my grandparents and said, "Listen, I've got something very important to tell you. Could you ask Aunt and Uncle to come over? I want to talk to the four of you together." I had no idea what he thought the announcement was. To say the least, sharing my life-changing decision with them didn't go very smoothly.

"Oh, so now it's you and Adolph Hitler," they said.

"What? What does Adolph Hitler have to do with anything?"

"Well, he was a Christian!"

"He was NOT a Christian."

"Well, he wasn't Jewish, he wasn't Muslim, so he was a Christian."

"What are you talking about? He might have been a Gentile but he wasn't a Christian!"

That was pretty much the end of the discussion. I think they would rather have had me come home and tell them that I had been using LSD five times a week, smuggling weed in from Amsterdam and almost getting arrested than tell them I believed in Jesus. When I got back to Cora's house, I was pretty discouraged. She said, "Honey, listen, you have to *pray* for these people that God will drop the scales from their eyes. That's what I was worried about. You were going in there with no prayer cover. We need to pray for them." She was a really wise, godly woman.

After I came to Christ, I started hitchhiking around the country with my dog. When we arrived in Washington, D.C., in the summer of 1971, I met Bob Porter, an ex-alcoholic and former semipro ballplayer. He gave all that up when he became a Christian and started a street-witnessing ministry. He introduced me to Bill Simmer, the leader of the Good News Mission in Arlington, Virginia. Bill was a strong believer in the importance of Bible education. I told him that I really felt God was calling me into ministry, and he said, "You need to go to seminary." I didn't even know what seminary was. "What do you do in seminary?" I asked. He told me that you learn Greek, Hebrew, exegesis (Bible interpretation), theology and how to preach. I thought that sounded awesome.

There was one right there in Washington, D.C., called Capital Bible Seminary. I went for an interview with the dean of the seminary with my Afro, a little goatee and wearing bell-bottoms.

"I really believe that God is calling me to seminary."

"Well . . . why don't we start part-time and see how it goes? Oh, and you have to get a haircut."

"Why do I have to get a haircut?"

"Because those are our rules. We have to be able to see your ears."

"Sir, I haven't seen my ears in years."

"Well, you're going to see them now if you are going to come here."

At that point in my life, that was a really big decision—whether I was going to get a haircut and go to seminary. Well, I got my hair cut and started part-time. I did well enough for them to allow me to study full-time. I was passionately in love with Hebrew, in particular, as well as Greek and exegesis. That led me to believe I should be a seminary teacher.

Another reason seminary was so great was that I met Brenda. She was an undergraduate student and I was in the graduate school. I had made a list of what I was looking for in a marriage partner. I had three columns: nonnegotiable, very important and nice but not necessary. As I began to get to know Brenda casually, I realized, *Wow, this girl has got everything on my list!* When I asked her out, I knew that if we ended up falling in love, she was a girl who would make a great marriage partner. We dated for three months and then I asked her to marry me. She said no! So I said, "Okay, I withdraw my offer. Let's keep dating and if I still want to marry you, I'll ask you again." She said, "Okay." We kept dating for a couple of more months and I asked her again; this time she said yes. We were engaged for a year while she finished school, and we got married in 1974.

Brenda was from a small town in Maryland, and my family and I were the first Jewish people she had met. She adjusted marvelously. It wasn't long before my family preferred her to me! I remember my grandfather telling her, "You know what, I like you better than I like him. If you get a divorce, I'm keeping you. He can go wherever he wants." Brenda is such a sweet, kind and gentle person that they took to her right away. The fact that she was a *shiksa* (a Gentile woman) was never an issue.

When I enrolled in seminary, my parents realized my Christianity was going to stick. They coped all right with it and never rejected me, but I don't think they were proud of me. When people asked my dad, "What does your son do?" he would say, "He's working on his

masters." He avoided telling them that I was at seminary
working on my masters in theology. If they asked him
what I was studying, he would reply, "I think religion."

After I graduated, I worked on my doctorate at Johns
Hopkins in Near Eastern studies and taught for five years
at Capital Seminary. Seminary is a great thing and I am so
grateful for my training. But I felt like God wanted me
more on the front line where the bullets were whizzing—
where I could preach the gospel directly to the people. In
1979 I told the dean, "I'm going to resign. I don't know
where I'm going yet, but I really believe God wants me to
lead a church somewhere." Not long after that, McLean
Bible Church contacted me. They didn't know that I had
made that decision. They just contacted me to see if I had
any interest in being the pastor there. That was in 1980,
and I have been their pastor ever since.

However, my Jewishness continued to be an
important part of my identity. And my desire to see my
Jewish family know the Messiah never waned. One of
the greatest privileges God has ever given me was
leading my dad to Jesus just before he died. He had a
heart condition and was taken to the hospital in
Charlottesville, North Carolina. By this time he had
already had three heart attacks. My mother called to tell
me, "Your dad's in the hospital with hepatitis. He's really
ill and you need to come and see him." She made it
sound so serious that I rushed down that day to see him,
praying all the way.

By this time I'd been a Christian for seven years. I
had shared Jesus with him multiple times over those
years, but he had routinely ignored me. In my frustration,
the Lord spoke to me and said, "Lon, remember what
Cora told you. It's prayer that will bring the power of the
Holy Spirit into his heart." So I began to talk less and
pray more for him—begging God to bring him to faith in

Jesus before the next heart attack killed him.

I walked into the hospital room and my dad was sitting bolt upright, eating a banana! I couldn't believe my mom had misled me and there he was, doing fine. I guess that's what comes from having a Jewish mother!

We started to talk about the weather and I could tell something was on his mind. After we exchanged a few more pleasantries, he said, "You know, Lon, I've been doing a lot of thinking lately."

"Well, Dad, thinking is good. It's good to think."

"I've been thinking a lot about all the stuff you've been telling me about Jesus."

Oh my, I thought, holding my breath.

"I am beginning to wonder if maybe everything you are telling me is right."

I couldn't believe what I was hearing. I had been praying for my dad every day, sometimes twice a day. And suddenly I wondered, *Could my prayers be answered?* I felt like calling the nurse and asking her to clear the bed in the next room for me!

Lord, please don't let me say something wrong here, I prayed silently.

"There is no doubt in my mind that I'm right," I told my dad. "But you've never been interested or wanted to talk about this. Why all of a sudden are you saying I'm right?"

"Well, Lon, I've got to tell you," he replied. "I know I'm a sick man, and I decided that I could find everything in Orthodox Judaism that you said you found in Jesus. So I started to religiously attend synagogue again. I went on Rosh Hashanah and fasted for Yom Kippur, looking to find some assurance about what was going to happen to me after I die." The idea of dying terrified him. After his third heart attack, my mom later told me that he would stay up all night walking the halls, terrified that if he fell asleep, he'd never wake up.

"I finally walked out of the synagogue after Yom Kippur services," he continued. "I stood on the front steps of the synagogue and said to myself, *I don't have any more assurance of what's going to happen to me after I die now than I did before I went through all that ritual. Maybe Lon is right.*"

"Dad, I am so sure I am right, it's not even funny," I said.

The next morning I had the privilege of getting down on my knees with my father, next to his hospital bed, and praying with him as he asked Jesus into his life. He died one week later, to the day. During that week, his number one issue was that he believed Jesus had given him the assurance of eternal life, but he did not want to stop being Jewish. I tried to explain, "Dad, you don't become a Gentile when you believe in Jesus! You're always Jewish! You just complete everything that being Jewish is all about!"

The last time I saw my father before he died, he was in intensive care, hooked up to a tracheal tube. He had suffered his fourth (and final) heart attack while still in the hospital. He wasn't able to talk and frantically wanted to tell me something. There was a piece of paper, covered in plastic, with the alphabet written on it, so that patients could spell out words. He reached for this piece of paper and spelled out "L-O-R-D" "A-N-D" "J-E-W." I knew he was saying, "Lon, I have the Lord in my life, but I'm still a Jew." It was so affirming to see that, even under all the sedatives, my dad had enough presence of mind to say, "I know exactly who I am, Lon, and I've got Jesus Christ in my life."

My brother was next to come to faith. I'd shared what I believe with him many times, but it was his wife, Patrice, who eventually led him to Christ. While visiting her sister in Texas, Patrice attended a revival meeting at her sister's church and asked Jesus into her life. When she came back home and shared the news, my brother also accepted Jesus as his Lord and Savior. To this day he is walking with the Lord.

My brother and I began to double-team my mom. She had been battling breast cancer for some time when my brother finally led her to a relationship with Jesus. He called me up and said, "You'll never guess what's happened. I've led Mom to Christ." I said, "That's awesome! I'm really glad you got to do it, since I led Dad to Christ." It was gracious of the Lord to give each of us one of them. Like my dad, she had been terrified of dying. Right after I hung up the phone, I called my mom and said, "I understand you have asked Jesus to be your Lord and Savior." She said, "Yes I did, and I know I am going to heaven now. Isn't that true?" And I said, "Oh Mom, that is so utterly true, it's not even funny." I had a wonderful time praying with her over the telephone. She died just a few weeks later.

I shared the gospel with my grandparents (my mom's parents) several times after that initial meeting in Portsmouth in 1971, but they both died without any outward indication that they had given their lives to Christ. My relationship with my aunt and uncle has been rocky ever since that first time I tried to share my faith with them and my grandparents. My aunt, my mom's sister, was in complete denial about my mom's (her sister's) decision to believe in Jesus, despite the fact that both my brother and I told her my mom had accepted Christ.

Several years ago, the University of North Carolina alumni magazine did a great article on my life, in which I mention that my mom came to Christ. My uncle, who is an alumnus, read it and went absolutely crazy. He told my aunt, who called the magazine and asked them to print a retraction and publicly announce that I'd lied. One of the editors called me and said, "We have a

problem. Your aunt is challenging the veracity of this part
of your story." I told the editor, "Well, call my brother
and ask him." So she did. She asked my brother to go
through the story. She called me back to say, "We are
satisfied that the story you gave us is the truth, and we
are not retracting anything."

At first I wasn't as proud of being a Jewish believer as
I should have been. Growing up, I saw a lot of hypocrisy
and artificiality in my Jewish community. My attitude
changed when I was in seminary and met the person
who started the school, George Miles. He had a
passionate love for Jewish people, which helped me
understand how special it was to be a Jewish believer in
Jesus. Later, I became aware of the ministry of Jews for
Jesus and became a member of their board in 1987. God
had called me to be a pastor, not a missionary, but being
involved with Jews for Jesus enabled me to contribute to
the ongoing cause of Jewish evangelism. By God's grace,
I continue to serve on the board of Jews for Jesus today,
and it has been a real lifeline in strengthening and
enhancing my Jewishness. I am proud to be part of Jews
for Jesus and proud to be a Jewish believer.

I am not sharing my story with you because I am
proud of the life I lived before I came to know Jesus. I
want you to get a sense of whom I was at age 21 when
God reached down and grabbed hold of my life. I was
not some nice person who suddenly decided to get
religious. I was living a lifestyle that was about as
separated from God as one could imagine. But I believe
that God deals with the desperate. It is not that God will
not deal with nondesperate people. The problem is that
most of the time nondesperate people aren't interested in
dealing with God. A pig never looks up until it is on its
back. And that pretty well describes where I was in 1971
when the Lord Jesus redeemed me.

I can look back now and see how God took all my sinful behavior and used it to bring me to Christ. However, I carry a lot of emotional and spiritual scars from that lifestyle. I forced my girlfriend to abort my first child during that time. There's a lot of pain and heartache from those days. So I don't recommend that anybody go through that process. As the apostle Paul said, "Should we keep on sinning, so that God's wonderful kindness will show up even better? No, we should not!" (Romans 6:1–2, Contemporary English Version).

As I write this, I am about to turn 60 years of age. I've been walking with the sweet Lord Jesus for 38 years. It has been the most amazing journey—taking me places that I could never have imagined in my wildest dreams, when the journey began so long ago on the streets of Chapel Hill.

As the years have gone by, God has graciously given four wonderful children to Brenda and me. As I write this in 2008, God had also given us two beautiful grandchildren. My oldest son, James, is a graduate of the U.S. Naval Academy (1999) and a medical doctor in the U.S. Navy. My middle son, Justin, is a graduate of Michigan Law School (2003) and works at a law firm in Chicago. My youngest son, Jon, played intercollegiate baseball at Johns Hopkins University (2008 graduate) and works in the Washington, D.C., area. By God's grace, all three boys are walking with the Lord and are married to wonderful believers. God also gave us a very special daughter, Jill, who has multiple disabilities. She is a direct blessing from the Lord and we love and treasure her deeply.

The Lord has been far better to me than I deserve. He has blessed me far out of proportion to my meager efforts to love and serve him. His faithfulness to me has exceeded by light-years my puny faithfulness (and many times, my unfaithfulness) to him.

But this is simply how God is! He is the Good Shepherd—the ultimate benevolent heavenly Father—the God of all faithfulness. His grace and mercy toward his children in Christ is measureless, and without limit or logic. God owes me nothing. He is not my debtor. He has outgiven me in every way, just as he promised in the Word of God: "He who did not spare His own Son, but delivered Him over for us all, how will He not also with Him freely give us all things? (Romans 8:32).

The most blessed day of my life was the day I surrendered my heart and life to Jesus the Messiah.

In closing, please let me say that I am convinced that the only way to have the assurance of eternal life, and the peace and joy we are all looking for, is to have a personal relationship with Jesus, the Messiah of Israel. He said, "I am the way and the truth and the life. No one comes to the Father except through me" (John 14:6).

If he is right, and I believe he is, then the only way to get that personal connectedness with God is through a relationship with Jesus. I tried everything else, with equal commitment, passion and openness to the idea that they were going to work. You can go and try them all if you want. I did, and I can tell you that the reason those things did not work is because none of them are the true way to God. But I can also tell you that if you give Jesus a sincere chance to prove himself to you, he will, as he did for me. Read the Bible. Read the New Testament. Read the Gospel of John, the Gospel of Matthew, and as you read them ask God if Jesus is really who he said he is. Say to God, as I did, "If Jesus is real and you are real, show me, and if you show me, I am willing to believe." And I can assure you, that if you mean business, God will reveal himself to you, just like he did to me.

I didn't grow up to be a doctor or a lawyer, but neither did I become a failure. In a sense, I became royalty, because I am related to the King of Kings. What Jewish parent or any parent could complain about that? ∎

MAKING SURE YOU ARE ONE OF GOD'S SHEEP

We've been talking about God's role as the Good Shepherd and our relationship to him as God's sheep for this entire book.

But it's important to ask, "Well, how does a person know if they're one of God's sheep?" It's important at this point that we stop for a moment and say that Lord is our personal shepherd IF we're one of his personal sheep.

So you might say, "Well, how does a person know if they're one of God's sheep?" Very simple. It's all about personal ownership by the shepherd.

You see, in David's times, sheep were not wild animals. They were domesticated animals that were valuable pieces of personal property in Israel. The shepherd *owned* his sheep. They were a personal asset, if you will.

Here in the state of Virginia, we have this dreadful thing called "personal property tax." The state of Virginia has a book that places a value on people's personal property, most notably motor vehicles, trailers and boats, and assesses an annual tax on them. My point is that if shepherds lived in Virginia today, the state would make them pay personal property tax on every one of their sheep!

For a shepherd in Israel, his sheep were the most valuable piece of personal property that he owned. They were more valuable than his tent or his house. A shepherd would buy his sheep at great expense. He owned every part of them. He owned their wool. He owned their fleece. He owned their offspring. He owned the meat on their bones should he choose to kill and eat them. And he would notch each one of his sheep's ears in his own special way so that everybody who walked by would know that *this* sheep belonged to *that* shepherd.

The Bible tells us clearly that every person alive is not one of God's personal sheep. Now this may come as a shock to many of us. We are used to hearing the Madison Avenue mantra, "Well, we're all God's children." The fact is, the Bible simply doesn't teach this. The Bible teaches that every human being is one of God's creatures, but not one of his personal sheep. Jesus said in John 10:26, "But you do not believe because you are not of My sheep." How much clearer could Jesus be? There are some people in this world who are "his sheep" and some people in the world who are not "his sheep."

To put it in terms of David's words here in the 23rd Psalm, the Bible teaches that not every human being qualifies to have God as their personal shepherd because not every human being qualifies as one of God's personal sheep. Jesus went on in John 10 to explain exactly who qualifies as his sheep. He said, "My sheep hear My voice, and I know them, and they follow Me;

and I give eternal life to them, and they will never perish" (John 10:27–28); and "I am the good shepherd, and I know My own and My own know Me" (John 10:14).

There are so many people who are trying to claim the blessings of the 23rd Psalm for their life when, in reality, this psalm doesn't belong to them yet. It doesn't belong to them yet because they have not qualified as one of God's personal sheep yet.

This psalm belongs to God's sheep and them alone. It belongs to those people whom God has bought with a price just as a shepherd buys his sheep with a price. The price we've been bought with is the blood of Jesus Christ, shed on the cross, to pay for our wrongdoings in the sight of a holy God. This psalm belongs to the people who have appropriated what Jesus did for them on the cross; who have put their full trust in his blood as their only payment for sin; who have taken Jesus Christ as their personal Savior and intentionally embraced him as the Lord and Master of their lives.

You see, for God to be our personal shepherd, we must first decide that we are going to be one of his personal sheep by making a 100 percent surrender of our lives to God's ownership, where he now owns our wool, our fleece, our offspring, the very meat on our bones if he wants it. If we want God to be our personal shepherd, this is the kind of business transaction we must first go through to become one of his personal sheep.

I want to urge you to make absolutely sure that you're one of God's sheep because you have embraced Jesus as your personal Messiah and Savior—because you are relying on his blood, shed on the cross, as your only payment for wrongdoing in God's sight and your only hope of entering heaven.

For you see, until you're one of God's sheep, this psalm is not for you. You cannot claim something that's not yours. But if you belong to Jesus, I want to tell you that this psalm is *your* property. You can write all over the top of it, "This is mine, all mine. Every promise in here is mine. Every assurance God gives in here is mine. It's all for me." And it is!

Lord Jesus, I come to you today because I want to become one of your personal sheep. I want the 23rd Psalm to be my property because you have become my personal heavenly shepherd.

And so today, I humble myself before you and admit that I am a sinner who stands rightfully condemned before your holiness. Today, I repent of my sins and I turn from them to you.

Today I embrace what Jesus did for me on the cross: shedding his blood to pay for my sin in your holy sight. I give up every other remedy for sin that I have ever trusted and I take refuge behind the blood of Jesus—plus nothing—as my full and external remedy for sin.

Today I surrender my life to you as my personal Lord and Savior. I abdicate the throne of my life to you, and I acknowledge your lordship over every portion of my life.

I ask you, in your mercy, to come into my life, to forgive my sins and to make me one of your personal sheep. I ask you to grant me eternal life and a secure place in heaven forever. I ask you to place the indwelling Holy Spirit inside me and to begin transforming my earthly life into something worth getting up for in the morning.

I surrender to you all that I am and all that I ever hope to be. You are the Master and I am honored to be your servant. You are the shepherd and I am grateful to be one of your personal sheep. In Jesus' name, Amen.